PREACHER

by E. F. Hallock

Foreword by Dr. Leroy Ford

PREACHER HALLOCK

by E. F. Hallock

Foreword by Dr. Leroy Ford

Wipf & Stock
PUBLISHERS
Eugene, Oregon

Wipf and Stock Publishers
199 W 8th Ave, Suite 3
Eugene, OR 97401

Preacher Hallock
All the Promises: The Remarkably inspiring autobiography
of one who believed in life direction through Bible promises
By Hallock, E. F.
Copyright©1976 by Hallock, E. F.
ISBN: 1-59752-694-0
Publication date 5/16/2006
Previously published by Acton House, 1976

Some of the material in this book has been previously published by
Broadman Press, under the title *Always in Prayer*.

DEDICATION

This book is lovingly dedicated to our daughter, Vera Beth Hallock Rose. She loved the Bible; she lived by its promises; she obeyed her Lord as he spoke to her from His Word. It inspired her prayer life; and it was, indeed, a lamp to her feet and a light to her path. Her faithfulness to the Lord is expressed in Paul's great affirmation, "To me to live is Christ."

And now in heaven she knows, "To die is to gain."

Foreword

Edgar F. (Preacher) Hallock would never think of himself as a spiritual giant. But those closest to him know it to be true. Future generations will place his name alongside giants like George Mueller and David Brainerd. Both influenced him greatly in his understanding of how prayer, Bible reading, and "all the promises" work together in shaping the spiritual life. But the Example of Examples, and the Influence of Influences on his spiritual life was the redeeming Christ revealed in God's Word.

Preacher Hallock tells in autobiographical form how one man of God listened and responded as God spoke through his Word. It reveals a man who saw prayer and Bible reading as inseparably linked—like two wings of an aircraft—one incomplete without the other. "But," he would say, "If for some reason I had to make a choice (which I cannot imagine having to do), I would choose Bible reading. It's more important that I hear what God says to me."

Preacher Hallock reads his Bible.—He used to say, "Read it through, write it down; pray it in; and live it out!"

To my knowledge, no source outside this book contains a permanent record of the extent to which his love for the Word caused him to read it. Characteristic modesty would never permit him to ponder the mathematics of how many times he had read the Bible through. So in early 1976, I drove to Norman, Oklahoma, for the specific purpose of obtaining this record for the encouragement of Christians everywhere.

A verbatim report of the conversation with him follows:

Question: What year was it that you started talking about getting church members to read the Bible through once a year?

Hallock: In 1922. That was at Nowata (Oklahoma). And then I came here you see. (First Baptist Church, Norman, Oklahoma). I just landed! I landed running!

Question: Have you read it through every year since then (1922 through 1976)?

Hallock: Yes, I have. At least twice.

Question: At *least* twice a year? (For fifty-four years.)

Hallock: Yes.

Question: You have a plan for reading the Old Testament and the New Testament some way in combination. . . .

Hallock: Well, I just read the whole thing straight through. I just start at Genesis and go straight through. Once in a while I may kind of try some other way, but I have found out this: that there is (and this is a theological term) a progressive unfolding of God as you read the Bible from Genesis to Revelation. I couldn't take it and write it out, but I can feel it, and I can somehow see it—how God has made himself known through the Scriptures to a person who will read it prayerfully. After a while you get so when you pick up the Bible that (I don't mean it's magic or a fetish or anything like that) you get so you feel like you're going in to talk to the Lord. And sometimes it's not too interesting reading, but even so, there's something about *that* reading that touches you.

* * *

Question: You probably won't want to answer this, but I'm going to ask it anyway.

Hallock: I'll answer it.

Question: Is that a promise? If you added up say, the pages and the time you have spent reading the Bible, how many readings through—the equivalent of "readings through"—do you suppose you have done in your lifetime?

Hallock: Oh, LeRoy, I wouldn't know how, because I read, oh I read separate books a number of times. Like the Gospel of John. One summer I read it through out loud forty-two times. And you take Paul's epistles. I've read them over and over and over until I knew them by heart, and then I'd forget them and read them again, and learn them over. And that's been true of the Psalms and there are certain Psalms that I forget. And I'm glad I forget them because that means that I have got to memorize them again! And when I memorize, I'm forced to face them and think!

I don't sleep very well at night now and some nights I

viii

take a little medicine, you know, to make me go to sleep, but it makes me stay awake! Like last night. So I just take the eighty-fourth Psalm and I'll go through it again and again. *It's just like walking around in a park!"*

Question: I remember one time you challenged the members of the church to read I Corinthians 13 fifty times in one week! (I also remember that he read the book of Philippians fifty times before going to teach it at First Baptist Church, Lawton, Oklahoma. And I remember that he memorized the entire book of Acts one summer and quoted it Sunday by Sunday in a series of sermons.)

* * *

Question: I was leading a conference not too long ago. I was telling about the fact that you had mentioned so many times that George Mueller had read the Bible through 200 times. I guess you got that out of his biography. And I remember telling them that I expected you had equalled that by this time.

Hallock: Well, I don't think so. George Mueller, the last 25 years of his life (he died at 91) read the Bible through four times a year.

Comment: That's a lot of reading!

Hallock: Yes. I did it one time—four times—and that is a lot of reading, especially when you have a busy pastorate to work in and all.

Those of us who know him best and who are not bound by modesty, do not hesitate to say that he has read the Bible through more often than that.

Preacher Hallock lives by God's promises in the Bible.— And that's what this book is about. To him, God's promises are sufficient even to the end of life. In the same conversation he said,

"I was just telling Mom this morning that at my funeral, I want Joe Henning to sing 'Jesus Loves Me, This I Know,' because *it says, 'the Bible tells me so'!* Faith! That's the only way I know I'm saved, *because the Bible tells me so.* I've done what the Bible says to do and I believe it and so I know I'm saved. You know, that's a tremendous thing— justified! That's a word I never have played around with much. But lately it's been in my mind a lot because I know that some of these days before long I'm going to be there. And I'm not going to have anything to stand on of my own,

ix

but I'll be justified! (long pause) Well, there's nothing like the Bible! (long pause) . . . I like to talk about the things of the Lord because they're my life. That's all I know to talk about."

Preacher Hallock understands the "stewardship of pain."—

"I think I've learned that the Lord runs this show—and I sure like to tell people that! Somebody the other day tried to tell me, 'Well, I just don't think it's right for God to give you cancer!" I said, 'Well, *He's running this show!* Not I!" I get a bang out of that! Well, I don't think He gave it to me. I think He let me have it because He knew that this was perhaps the final opportunity (for me) to glorify Him. And after all, that's what we're here for. The total result, the summing up of all that we are has for its purpose the revealing of God to the people—to the world. I don't know of anything that helps people to see any more than glorifying God in your suffering."

It was my joy to work with Preacher Hallock as minister of education at First Baptist Church, Norman, Oklahoma, from 1950 to 1956. What an honor now to have him and Mrs. Hallock ask me to work this manuscript through to publication. I would wish for every church staff member a pastor-staff member relationship such as we enjoyed. At Christmas, 1954, he presented me with a new copy of the American Standard Version of the Bible. On the flyleaf he wrote "2 Cor. 1:20-22." In part, it reads: "Now he that establisheth us with you in Christ, and annointed us, is God." He even had a promise about our work together! And they were golden years.

LeRoy Ford, 1976

Addendum: During Preacher's pastorate all church publ cations, including letterheads, carried at the top of the item this verse from Zechariah 4:6: "Not by might, nor by power, but by My Spirit, says the Lord of hosts." He believed it meant what it said. No facet of the work of the church and the denomination would be accomplished by political strategies.

Preacher's utter dependence on the Spirit was behind his refusal many times to have his name placed in nomination for the office of President of the Baptist General Convention of Oklahoma. He would have to be sure that no human power structure or political force was behind such a move. (For the same reason Preacher hesitated before accepting an honorary doctorate from Oklahoma Baptist University.)

At a convention meeting in Tulsa in the fifties, John Shelton, then pastor of Trinity Baptist Church in Norman, along with others approached me with a request. They asked whether I would talk to Preacher to help get his permission for them to submit his name to the Convention for the office of President. They wanted me to assure him that there was no political motive behind the move. They felt the Convention needed as President a man of prayer, piety, and submission to the leadership of the Spirit. Our hotel rooms adjoined, so I talked to Preacher. Then I left. When I saw him again, he said, "It's all right." The Convention elected him as President.

Preacher believed that the breaking of fellowship in a church or denominational group resulted in the loss of spiritual power. I learned much from him in this respect. A church in our association was conducting a premillennial rally lead by a nationally known premillennialist. The pastor of the church looked to Preacher as his mentor. One day Preacher said to me, "I guess we ought to go to the meeting today." He felt that the promising young pastor might not understand his absence from the conference.

Arriving late, we slipped into the back row in the packed auditorium. After the guest had spoken, the young pastor expressed pleasure at Preacher's presence, then added, "I want to ask Preacher Hallock to close this session with prayer." Preacher's prayer, as usual, focused on Christ and the promise.

On the way home, Preacher said to me, "LeRoy, I wish he hadn't asked me to do that." Although Preacher held to the premillennial viewpoint, he said, "I'm afraid people will associate me with those who make a viewpoint on the millennium a test of fellowship." He added, "Differences of viewpoint on the millennium are not adequate grounds for breaking fellowship."

Preacher believed that the Bible's purpose was to reveal Christ to man. Much of his prayer time was spent trying to know Christ in a more personal way. He told me one day of such a prayer experience. It happened on the second floor office at the rear of the original brick sanctuary at the corner of Webster and Comanche Streets in Norman, Oklahoma. During the intense prayer experience his heart and mind had sensed an unusual vision of the glory and majesty of Jesus. After the meaningful prayer time, he lifted his eyes. His eyes fell on the the picture "The Head of Christ."

"As I looked at it," he told me, "my heart sank. I felt ill." The painter's attempt to create a visual image of the Christ had fallen so far short of the vision Preacher had experienced that, he said, "I felt nauseated."

One of my most precious possessions is a letter Preacher wrote to me shortly after the meeting of the Southern Baptist Convention in Kansas City in 1963. The Convention at that meeting endorsed the 1963 statement of "The Baptist Faith and Message." I was in a hotel editing manuscripts for *Baptist Adults* and *Baptist Young Adults* published by the Training Union Department of The Baptist Sunday School Board where I worked. The units of study dealt with Baptist Doctrine. I waited minute-by-minute for the Convention's action so that I could be sure the units of study reflected the new statement. I did not see Preacher. After the Convention, he wrote me on May 22, 1963:

> As you well know, if all our preachers, and that is pretty much what the convention is, preachers, would major in Bible reading with the first emphasis on finding the mind of God as they read, and walking with God in this experience of reading, we would come to a ground of unity far superior to that of doctrine alone. I would not minimize the place nor the value of doctrine and theology. I believe that they are essential and fundamental but without the

other experience of God through the Book, theology and doctrine are barren.

Preacher believed the Bible was the record of God's revelation of himself in Christ.

Preacher had a word for those who engage in endless discussion on inspiration as it relates to the Scriptures. A sermon illustration went like this: Three starving men are marooned on an island. A crate of food washes ashore. The men starve to death arguing over where it came from.

Preacher and Dr. Frank Leavell were instrumental in establishing Baptist student ministries on college and university campuses. Preacher had a simple philosophy on the work of the Baptist Student Union. "The work of the Baptist Student Union is the work of the local church," he said. The Hallock Chair of Student Ministries at Southwestern provides opportunities for seminary students to prepare for that ministry.

For years I encouraged Preacher to put in writing his concept of living by Bible promises. After we came to Fort Worth where I taught in the School of Religious Education at Southwestern Baptist Theological Seminary, one day the doorbell rang. Preacher and Mrs. Hallock were at the door. Preacher handed me a manuscript, "Well, LeRoy, here it is," he said. "I'll leave it to you to get it published. I just don't feel like dealing with the details."

Preacher's original title for this manuscript was *All the Promises,* but the publisher changed the title to *Preacher Hallock.* Preacher felt the new title drew attention to him, not to Christ as revealed in the book.

LeRoy Ford, 2006

Reflections on My Dad

Ardelle Hallock Clemons

When I was growing up my Dad was the light of my life. He was a true father who led me to be in touch with our Heavenly Father. He was a rock of stability as well as a font of fun and joy for me and my siblings.

He was always present to us kids. As busy and in demand as he was, we had access. When we needed help—whether advice, consolation or money—we could talk to Dad. We didn't always get the money, because he made so little. But we always knew he loved us and was there for us. We got him. The world knew him as "Preacher" but we knew him as Dad.

He had a stress-related illness in mid-life. After that, his being there for us became even "moreso." He realized his priorities needed rearranging, and he did just that.

My father was a spiritual guide who practiced what he preached. He taught us by precept and example to trust God for leadership and for daily strength. He was a man of prayer. He devoured the Bible in the wee hours of the morning and throughout the day. The Scripture was truly a lamp for his feet and a light for his pathway.

Dad was playful! He was fun to be with, lighthearted, and had a wonderful sense of humor. We played a lot as a family. We loved that and we loved him! He also savored those times. I can still hear his hearty laugh at his own and others' humor.

My Dad was easy to relate to. We could approach him and he would receive us warmly. He listened with his inner ears. He gave us a powerful model of what we could be as Christ's followers. He helped us make our God relationship rich and real.

We weren't required to fit a mold as "PKs." We knew he wanted us to become genuine, authentic people. He encouraged us to be the persons God planned for us to be. He showed us how to live out our calling as followers and ministers for God.

LeRoy Ford has done a superb job of picturing the man he worked with for all those years. Dad loved LeRoy like a son and related to him as a friend and partner in ministry. I would love to hear "Dad's" side of the story about LeRoy. He placed deep respect and confidence in LeRoy. I know my Dad would be pleased to know that he is republishing this wonderful book.

Table of Contents

Introduction: This Is My Story

Christianity is widely thought of as a code of morals, a set of ethical principles, a great program of social action. To be a Christian, for many, is to embrace this moral code, adopt these ethical principles, and work at accomplishing the goals of social betterment among men. But to be a Christian is vastly more than any or all of these things. These things are the fruits. To be a Christian in accordance with the meaning of the New Testament is to receive the redeeming Christ of Calvary's cross and of the empty garden tomb. He died to expiate our sin. He was "raised for our justification" (Rom. 4:25, ASV). We become Christians when we receive him as Savior and Lord.

For nineteen years I was a professed Christian striving to practice Christ's moral and ethical teachings. I gave myself to the service of Christ to make his principles effective in individual and community life both near and far.

I seriously began this Christian life when I was fourteen years old. I heard a message which said, "A day of judgment before the Lord is coming. At that time all your sins will be displayed before you and God, just as if written on a great white sheet."

This was extremely disturbing. The messenger continued by saying, "If you will trust Christ, he will clean that white sheet of its black record, and you can begin again." I was convinced; and when the invitation hymn was sung, I walked down the aisle and fulfilled the conditions set before me, the best I knew. Now I would keep that sheet clean by clean, pure living. And I worked the works as I saw them. It was clear to me that I must be good and maintain that striving after goodness if I would go to heaven. I heard a sermon in a neighboring church that made me greatly aware that I could be a saved person today; but if I sinned, I was lost and must get saved again. This was enforced by a vivid illustration.

The preacher, a woman, had in her hand a large horseshoe

1

magnet. Across its two ends was a bar of iron with a string around it. On the string were some objects that symbolized our sins. The magnet was Christ, and the bar of iron was the Christian. In that hour the Christian was I, and the sins were mine, also. She lifted the magnet—it held you and all your sins until the last, symbolized by a plug of chewing tobacco. When she undertook to lift that, its weight added to the others pulled you loose and you were lost.

That illustration really formed my doctrine of salvation. I refined my doctrine, but retained the fact. I believed that I had to earn eternal life; therefore, I would deserve to be saved.

For nineteen years I worked all the works I knew. I read the Bible. I prayed much. I faithfully attended church services, I tithed what I earned, I taught Sunday School classes. I followed Jesus in his teachings. I led prayer meetings; I sang in the choir. I did all I knew and tried to find more to do. Because of these works I would be saved.

Yes, I loved Jesus! He was my ideal, and at the age of twenty I concluded he was calling me to be a preacher. The driving motive was to please him with my works, so that he would not deny me entrance into heaven.

In my college days I began to be an intellectualist and a liberal in doctrine. In fact I became a modernist. As a modernist my Bible, my praying, my Christ were devalued, but not my belief in salvation by works. Of course modernism taught me that hell was a myth long since abandoned by intelligent people. There might be a heaven; but if I maintained a high level of moral living and social service, heaven would take care of itself. If there were no heaven, then this was the best life anyway. All this modernistic development came in my seven years of college and seminary education. But, I was not lost because of modernism. I was a modernist because I was lost.

At twenty-eight I became pastor of the First Baptist Church in Pittsburg, Kansas. Immediately I entered a totally different spiritual and intellectual climate. This was an industrial town of eighteen thousand people in the center of a prosperous coal-producing region. The church membership was spiritual and warm. In that church God began to melt away my "pride of learning" and my pride in my "modernistic progressiveness."

I was led to return to the belief that Jesus did rise from the dead. That was a big step. Then, by the prayers of the people, our sixteen-month-old baby was brought back to life from the very door of death. This caused me to begin to make prayer vital. An intensive three-month study of Paul's Roman epistle almost gave me the saving life; an every-night prayer meeting for five weeks acted as the great irrigation of a prepared field; and at last the light came.

Evangelist T. T. Martin came for an evangelistic revival. His associate, E. A. Petroff, preceded him and preached for ten nights to the church. Then Brother Martin came to preach the gospel to the lost.

In each message he quoted these words from Titus 2:13-14, ASV: "Our Savior Jesus Christ; who gave himself for us, that he might redeem us from all iniquity." Then he would ask, "For how many of our sins did he die? For ALL of them—past, present, and future, clear up to the time you die."

In five sermons he must have said these words at least fifty times. It never occurred to me that they carried a message to my spirit. If I had been confronted by someone saying, "This is your message," I would have said, "No, not for me."

As the end of his message in the fifth service came near, with surprising and jolting unexpectedness those words exploded in my soul,—"for how many of our sins did he die? For ALL of them—past, present, and future, clear up to the time you die." The Holy Spirit removed the veil of blindness, and I saw it like the glory of the rising sun. Sudden overpowering conviction seized me! Now I knew I was lost! Although I had followed Jesus, I had never known him as Redeemer, Savior, and expiator of my sins. That night hell was my destination! All this and more came with such clearness and power that I was stunned.

The next twenty-four hours were hours of miserable unbelief and stabbing conviction of my "self-salvation" as opposed to the amazing grace of the Lord.

I went to church the next evening in spiritual and mental agony. I had come to know what I should do! I must receive this Redeemer for all sin and make a public confession. But pride of position, pride of learning, pride of pursuing eternal life by works, this pride made me think, "If I walk the aisle to the altar, confessing my lostness and a faith in Jesus as Redeemer, the people will think I have lost my mind, and I will lose my job."

3

But the Holy Spirit stayed with me. As I debated what to do, he said in my inner being, "It's tonight or never for you!" My pride said, "The people will think you have lost your mind." Presently the Spirit spoke again, "It's tonight or never for you!" Again I demurred. I let my pride assert itself. But the Holy Spirit in faithfulness spoke a third time, "It's tonight or never for you!"

Then I knew and said to myself, "This is God speaking to me! I don't care what they think." The sermon was ended; before Brother Martin could give the invitation, I was there confessing, "I saw last night that Jesus died for all my sins, past, present, and future, clear up to the time I die. And I have just received Him as my Redeemer and Savior."

"This is my story." Once I gave myself to God to earn his favor and life by my works. Now I have received from him the revelation of his grace and the gift of eternal life.

My outward life, to the average person, did not change a lot. But to the spiritual man there was evident a new motive, a new love for the Lord, and a new power—the indwelling Spirit. I was born again.

But now—what next? God delivered me from liberalism in my beliefs and gradually healed the painful scars. I was saved Tuesday night, November 21, 1921. On Christmas Day, five weeks later, the First Baptist Church of Nowata, Oklahoma, called me about becoming their pastor. I said no. But God changed my "no" to his "yes." There in Nowata he led me into great fellowship with himself in Bible reading and prayer.

After twenty-one months, he moved me to Norman, to the First Baptist Church. Here he taught me that obedience to his will is the open door to all his riches and the new life of walking with him in his Word.

"Turst and obey": this is the song of my life; and "Standing on the Promises" is my song of victory in Jesus.

My Arabia: Nowata, Oklahoma

Paul wrote, "when he . . . was pleased to reveal his Son to me, . . . [I did not] go up to Jerusalem . . . but I went away into Arabia" (Gal. 1:15-17, RSV). Apparently he was in Arabia pondering the great reversal of his life, from persecutor of the church to preacher of the gospel. Also he was recalling the Old Testament message of sacrifices for sin, of the prophets, of the Suffering Servant, and more. Then when the time was ended in Arabia, he became the tireless missionary of Jesus the Christ.

Many of God's gospel preachers have been reversed, some gently, some violently, from a life of self and sin to a new life in Jesus and a life of dedicated service for Christ toward men.

My salvation experience was just such a reversal for me. I was totally changed from trust in "salvation by works" to "salvation by grace." I was completely reversed from my theological and doctrinal directions of modernistic liberalism to the theology and doctrines of a divinely inspired Bible. I had to understand the change and the things I was to believe, to teach and to preach. So God gave me an "Arabia" in Nowata, Oklahoma.

I became a zealous believer and preacher of the gospel as set forth in 1 Corinthians 15:1-4. I heard a layman preach on the theme, "Tampering with the Formula." He said the chemical formula for water is H_2O. Tamper with the formula and add another molecule of oxygen; now you have hydrogen-peroxide. Add a little more and set up the formula H_2SO_4; then you have sulphuric acid. The unchangeable, irreducible formula for the gospel is "that Christ died for our sins in accordance with the scriptures, that he was buried, that he was raised on the third day in accordance with the scriptures" (1 Cor. 15:4, RSV).

In Nowata I studied that gospel until I began to know its great redemptive power for sinners. I saw men saved, and my own salvation gripped me more and more. I became an avid reader of the Bible. God moved me out of an overly busy pastorate in Pittsburg, Kansas, to a town one-third the size of Pittsburg and to a church of half the membership. Why? That I might have time for prayer and the Bible. I obeyed his call.

We had a good church program in Nowata. But my personal program was to master the Bible. I discovered the complete adequacy of my Teacher, the Holy Spirit. He taught me. He interpreted to me and led me continually.

I read the Bible through several times, and from that experience was formed the pattern of my life in relation to the Bible all these years. I set out to read it two or three times a year. I have done that these fifty-two years and plan to do so till God calls me home.

That summer, 1922, I read an interview given by G. Campbell Morgan. He was asked how he got ready to teach a Bible book. He said, "I read it out loud fifty times. Then I study it verse by verse and many of its words and truths. Then I make an outline. After that I go to the commentaries. Having done all this, the commentaries add very little."

I was inspired by this account; so I undertook to read the Gospel of John fifty times out loud. I discovered that it was a colossal task. But that experience also set another pattern for me. I have learned that repeated readings of Bible passages, long or short, are extremely enlightening.

Here in Nowata I was also led to read books that dealt with doubt, agnosticism, atheism, and various forms of unbelief. I often wondered why the Lord had allowed me to become a modernist. But there in my "Arabia" he completely removed my modernism and made me ready for work of which at that time I was not informed.

Then I received a letter from the First Baptist Church of Norman that changed all the future. It said, "This is one of five letters we are sending to five preachers asking them to appear before us with a view to a call." I can't explain it, but I had not finished reading it before I knew I was to be the pastor they would call. That was deep conviction given by the Lord who was leading me. And so it proved. Here in Norman is the University of Oklahoma. As I ministered to these hundreds of college students, I understood my years of modernism. I saw that God had specially prepared me for this ministry.

Out of "Nowata, my Arabia," he brought me to Norman to proclaim the gospel of God and to challenge Christians to know their God by personal reading and appropriation of the Scriptures. I have a fellow feeling for Paul when he wrote to Timothy, "I thank him who has given me strength for this, Christ Jesus our Lord, because he judged me faithful by appointing me to his service, though I formerly blasphemed and persecuted and insulted him; but I received mercy because I had acted ignorantly in unbelief, and the grace of the Lord overflowed for me with the faith and love that are in Christ Jesus" (1 Tim. 1:12-14, RSV).

Jesus' word in John 7:38 is the expression of my experience: "He who believes in me, as the scripture has said, 'Out of his heart shall flow rivers of living water.'"

He Leadeth Me

"He leadeth me," wrote David, the psalmist. He sought for and received the Lord's leadership in both his personal and his public life as king of Israel. After the death of Saul, although David knew that he was the Lord's man, anointed to be king, he "inquired of the Lord, 'Shall I go up into any of the cities of Judah?' And the Lord said to him, 'Go up.' David said, 'To which shall I go up?' And he said, 'To Hebron' " (2 Sam. 2:1, RSV). It was David's practice to seek God's leading.

The most dramatic experience of divine leadership ever given to any people came to Israel after they were delivered from Egypt. "And the people of Israel journeyed from Rameses to Succoth, about six hundred thousand men on foot, besides women and children" (Ex. 12:37, RSV). "And they moved on from Succoth. . . . And the Lord went before them by day in a pillar of cloud to lead them along the way, and by night in a pillar of fire to give them light, that they might travel by day and by night; the pillar of cloud by day and the pillar of fire by night did not depart from before the people" (Ex. 13:20-22, RSV).

Leadership, perfect leadership, is offered by our Lord to every person who has received him, the Savior and Lord of life. The leadership of "cloud and fire" was a corporate leadership; it was also individual and personal in that each could go along or go against. (An illustration of going against was Korah's rebellion, Num. 16.)

Today we experience corporate leadership in our churches and in denominational organizations. If our daily personal experience of the Lord's leading is clear, and if we are persons who seek to know and do God's will without reservations or hesitations, we will find his leadership in his body, the church, as it works out its God-given task.

I suppose most people live a lifetime without ever once having thought that the God who created them and redeemed them has some good ideas for their profit in living and working. They may confer with intimate friends for counsel, but seldom, if ever, with the God of life and love.

God said to Israel, "I know the plans I have for you" (Jer. 29:11, RSV). This is true of all God's children. In the American Standard Version, that line reads, "For I know the thoughts I think toward you, saith Jehovah." In an hour of spiritual and financial uncertainty, the Lord spoke from his Book these words to me. There was a divine finality in their assurance, and I received them as his way in which I should go. For all the years "his plans, his thoughts" have been utterly sufficient.

No Christian, no true believer, need ever to walk in darkness, astray from the path. Some do, but they choose to do so. Or perhaps they use none of God's means with which to find the way; they depend on their own understanding (Pro. 3:5).

For more than seventy years I have sought and received God's gracious guidance. That does not say that I have always obeyed his guiding word. But the Lord never failed me. When I was faithless, he was faithful, and in the end his will was always done.

The psalmist David spoke for each of us when he wrote, "He leadeth me." By his indwelling Holy Spirit God has led me. Sometimes he has led by circumstances and prayer; sometimes by consecrated human counselors; sometimes by abiding spiritual conviction; and always in connection with believing prayer and unshaken confidence in his words of promise, rebuke, or command from the Bible.

Sometimes a person does what Gideon did. He "put out a fleece." He told the Lord, "I am laying a fleece of wool on the ground. If, in the morning, the fleece is wet and the ground dry, then I shall know that thou wilt deliver Israel by my hand as thou hast said." God did what Gideon asked— Gideon got a bowl of water out of the fleece, and all around the ground was dry. But Gideon was not satisfied; so he said, "Let the fleece be dry and the ground wet." And God did it.

Before one undertakes to "put out a fleece," he should read all of Judges 6-7. For me, my years of walking with the Lord have shown me that I am safely in his will through prayer and Bible reading and the promises God gives.

"He leadeth me!" This is a grand declaration of faith and fact.

"All the way my Savior leads me,
What have I to ask beside?"

"All The Promises"

When I was still quite inexperienced in walking with the Lord in his promises, our church was seeking to call an educational director. One visited us and liked us and indicated that he would prayerfully consider our call.

Then, almost as an afterthought, I said, "Be sure to find a promise from the Lord before you decide."

He asked, "What's a promise?"

I was amazed at this question, because I thought that everybody lived by the promises of God. I explained God's promises. I urged him to seek the Lord's will and a promise prayerfully.

Three or four days passed. Then a letter came saying, "Yesterday my wife and I took the afternoon off, shut ourselves up at home, and spent the afternoon in prayer. We believe it is God's will that we accept your call." Of course we rejoiced.

At the Wednesday night prayer meeting in his church, he presented his resignation. His church said, "No, no, no. You stay here; we'll raise your salary; we'll build the new educational building and rent a better house for you."

The next morning I got this word from him, "If you ever prayed for anyone, pray for us the next few hours."

God had given me a promise and I was confident that he was coming. The promise said so. But the day following his request for prayer, I received his word: "We have decided to stay here."

After an afternoon of prayer they had said, "It is God's will to come." Now they said, "We are staying here."

I fell into a deep, dark spiritual pit of doubt about God's promises. My concern was not that he was not coming, but that my promise had failed. As I sat in my gloomy doubt, after about three hours these words, "All the promises"— began to knock at the door of my brain. The words came several times. I didn't know where to look for them. After a brief search I found them and some more. "For all the promises of God in him are yea, and in him Amen, unto the glory of God by us" (2 Cor. 1:20). My doubts lifted like a fog before the morning sun.

Apparently this man had been influenced by the promises of his church; but they kept none of their promises, and in six months he moved. As long as I had any knowledge of his movements, he was moving about once a year.

The ground of our trust in God is his promises. Trust in God apart from his promises is vague and uncertain. For our trust in God is simply our heart acceptance, for ourselves, of the things he has promised and commanded and given. As the hymn so aptly says, "'Tis so sweet to trust in Jesus, just to take him at his word."

The whole human race is living under a promise of God, although most are not aware of it. God said to Noah in Genesis 9:13-17 (RSV), "I set my bow in the cloud, and it shall be a sign of the covenant between me and the earth. When I bring clouds over the earth and the bow is seen in the clouds, I will remember my covenant which is between me and you and every living creature of all flesh; and the waters shall never again become a flood to destroy all flesh. When the bow is in the clouds, I will look upon it and remember the everlasting covenant between God and every living creature of all flesh that is upon the earth."

We thank God and praise Him for this promise when we see His bow in the clouds.

Abraham is the Old Testament's amazing man of promise. At the age of seventy-five, he emerges on the stage of history as a man of faith with a great promise, in fact, with a package of promises. How long he had lived by faith we do not know; but he was mature enough in his walk with Jehovah that it is written about him, "By faith Abraham obeyed when he was called to go out to a place which he was to receive as an inheritance; and he went out, not knowing where he was to go" (Heb. 11:8, RSV).

That package of promises said that he, a seventy-five-year-old man with a sixty-five-year-old wife, would have a son; and a great nation would grow from that son. Said God, "I will bless you, and make your name great, so that you will be a blessing" (Gen. 12:2, RSV). And the great comprehensive promise was, "I will bless them that bless thee, and him that curseth thee will I curse: and in thee shall all the families of the earth be blessed'' (Gen. 12:3, ASV).

He was to go "unto the land that I will show thee." God's promises grew from the promise in Genesis 13:15, "All the land which thou seest to thee will I give it" (ASV), to the vast promise in Genesis 15:18 (ASV), "Unto thy seed have I given this land, from the river of Egypt unto the great river, the river Euphrates."

Abraham saw the beginning of the fulfillment of these promises in the birth of his son Isaac. But he "died in faith, not having received the promises, but having seen them and greeted them from afar" (Heb. 11:13, ASV).

In the following centuries Joshua, David, Solomon, and others declared that not one thing had failed of all that was promised, but that all had come to pass. And we look to Jesus as the great fulfillment of Old Testament promises.

As I look back over more than seventy years of walking with the Lord "in the light of his word," I testify that God still speaks personally to his children from his Book, the Bible, by commands, exhortations, warnings, and promises. When the Lord speaks in and from his Word, it is personal and alive and perennial.

The lessons in a ten-year-old Sunday School department had been concerned with the confrontation of Moses with the Lord in the bush that burned and was not consumed. The children, impressed that God spoke from the burning bush, asked their teacher a proper question, "Why don't we have burning bushes today?"

I was invited to visit the department with the idea that I would answer their question. My reply was: "We do have 'burning bushes' today. We don't see them because we are not looking for them, and we don't hear God speaking because we are not listening."

I reminded the children of Samuel, who was about their age. A voice called, "Samuel." He thought Eli had called him, but Eli said, "No, go back to bed." The voice called a second and a third time, "Samuel, Samuel"; and in perfect obedience the boy ran to Eli to answer him. Finally Eli said, "If he calls again, say, 'Speak, Lord, thy servant is listening.'"

If we prayerfully read our Bibles with "eyes that see" and hearts that listen and obey, God speaks to us.

He speaks to us in teachings about love in our hearts, honesty in school examinations, kindness and forgiveness to those who hurt us, and many such good thoughts. If we are obedient in these things, then sometime when we have a need or a problem for which we are seeking help in prayer, God will give a word that fits our need and us, as we read our Bible.

For example, I was twenty years old. For two summers I had gone five hundred miles away from home and church to work. I did not go to church during those periods, and I neglected private prayer and my Bible. Those were unhappy summers. But when I returned in the autumns to my church, I rededicated myself, and joy came again.

But now, at age twenty, I was going away from home again, and that world far from my church looked to me like a burning, barren desert. I was full of dread as I faced it.

In my daily Bible reading was the eighth chapter of Acts. I came to verse 26, "And the Angel of the Lord spoke unto Philip, saying, 'Arise and go toward the south unto the way that 'goeth down from Jerusalem unto Gaza: the same is desert" (ASV). The Lord took those last four words, "The same is desert," and said to me, "If Philip could lead the Ethiopian eunuch to know and receive Jesus as Savior in the desert, then surely you can serve Jesus in Topeka, your desert."

That gave me peace and a call. He led me to the church where he wanted me. There I worked for nearly a year with more than sixty boys and girls from ten to fifteen years of age. My desert "rejoiced and blossomed as the rose."

In the years that followed, I continued reading my Bible, and I grew in my prayer life. Always I found help from the Lord in the truths he gave me. But it was a dozen years before I was given another specific promise for a specific need. Meanwhile I apparently found adequate help and guidance in the promises that are universally available to every believing child of God.

There are at least two kinds of promises in general. First are the verses and passages of Scripture that we normally claim as we read the Bible. They are spiritually ours; we may not comprehend and enjoy their riches to all their fulness, but they do sustain and strengthen us. The multitude of these promises is great. They are sure and ours for the taking, like food prepared and placed before us on the dinner table. "Help yourself" is the rule and practice.

As illustrative of such promises, I mention three or four. There is Philippians 4:13 (RSV), "I can do all things in him who strengthens me." There is Romans 8:28 (RSV), "We know that in everything God works for good with those who love him, who are called according to his purpose." And multitudes have claimed Psalm 23 and its many promises, and living by them, have walked following "the Lord, my shepherd." Available always is Matthew 6:33, "Seek ye first the kingdom of God, and his righteousness; and all these things shall be added unto you."

Such promises are innumerable. Those who trust and obey, faithfully, prayerfully reading the Bible, will find them and rejoice.

Second are the kinds of promises that speak to us when we have a specific problem, for whose solution God sees fit to give us a special verse or verses.

It is of these I am writing in particular. Two of them have been narrated in this chapter. Others will follow.

God's Word—Living—Active

"Seek ye the Lord while he may be found, call ye upon him while he is near: let the wicked forsake his way, and the unrighteous man his thoughts: and let him return unto the Lord, and he will have mercy upon him; and to our God, for he will abundantly pardon.

"For my thoughts are not your thoughts, neither are your ways my ways, saith the Lord. For as the heavens are higher than the earth, so are my ways higher than your ways, and my thoughts than your thoughts. For as the rain cometh down, and the snow from heaven, and returneth not thither, but watereth the earth, and maketh it bring forth and bud, that it may give seed to the sower, and bread to the eater: so shall my word be that goeth forth out of my mouth: it shall not return unto me void, but it shall accomplish that which I please, and it shall prosper in the thing whereto I sent it" (Isa. 55:6-11).

Verses 10-11 tell us that, just as surely as God's natural laws of rain and snow perform their appointed purpose, his word accomplishes his purpose and prospers in the work which he sent it to do. If we consistently used God's word and depended upon God to make it prosper, again and again we would see the glory of the Lord.

On Mother's Day, 1945, God's power had been manifested in our services. The people left rejoicing, and so did I.

I was about to enter my car and drive home when the church custodian ran up to me and said, "There's a man in the church who would like to speak to you." I found him, concerned and wistful, in the front of the auditorium. All others had gone. He was a Lt. Commander from the Norman naval base and director of the Gremlin band. Later I learned from my young people that he was nationally known as director of a radio orchestra.

I asked him, "Do you want to talk to me?" He nodded his head yes. I saw that he was emotionally disturbed.

16

I asked, "Do you want to talk to me about becoming a Christian?" Again he nodded.

I invited him to be seated, but he said, "I can't stay now. I am due at the base for duty in fifteen minutes. But may I come to your house on Thursday afternoon at 3:30? I will have forty-five minutes."

I said, "Yes, do come." he thanked me and left.

Promptly at 3:30 on Thursday he came. Almost immediately he said, "I've got a lot of questions I want to ask you. First, how do you know there is a God?"

I answered, "I don't want you to think I am answering lightly, but that is the easiest question you could ask me. I know there is a God because he answers my prayers, and I have a record of them."

Then I told him of specific prayers and specific answers. After each narration he exclaimed, "Well, I'll be darned!" I assure you that his "I'll be darned" was as reverent as any "Amen" that I have heard.

The forty-five minutes slipped by quickly, and he rose to go. He asked, "May I come back next Thursday at this time?"

I said, "Yes, and I want you to take this little Navy New Testament—I have a paper clip here (John 3:1-18). I'd like you to read these eighteen verses after praying this prayer— 'Lord, help me to understand and believe.' Do it over many times—a hundred or two hundred—many times."

He replied, "Sir, I'll do it."

For the next five Thursdays he came, and for the next five Sundays he attended the Sunday morning services. He was twenty-five years old and had attended church only twice in his whole life.

On the sixth Sunday morning the congregation was gone and I was leaving when I saw him walking toward me. As he came, he said, "Sir, I'm a Christian this morning."

I said, "Oh! Wonderful! Tell me what happened."

He said, "Last night I could not sleep. I had read those verses, just as you told me—many, many times. Again I prayed as I read them, but I could not sleep. So I dressed and at 2:00 A.M. I started walking the streets and praying. After what seemed a long time, I came to a church. I wondered if the door was unlocked. It was, and I went in. I kneeled by a bench, and I cried, 'O Lord Jesus, won't you please come into my heart?' And, sir, he came in."

I rejoiced with him; we talked awhile, and I inquired if he would come and confess his faith and join the church.

He replied, "I am on duty tonight, and I am being shipped out Tuesday morning."

God said of his word, "It shall accomplish that which I please, and prosper in the thing whereto I sent it."

Here was a young man reared in Brooklyn, New York, twenty-five years old, who had been to church only twice in his life. On Mother's Day, 1945, he visited the First Baptist Church in Norman, Oklahoma. A young woman had invited him. He was a man of the world, with no prior concern for the things of God. He said that as he sat in the worship service that morning, "something happened" to him. The Holy Spirit had touched him, with the result that he came to me, the pastor, a total stranger to him.

The leading of the Spirit was evident in the request that he read over and over John 3:1-18, and even more evident in his ready willingness to do as requested. Then, of course, the glorious power of the word of Christ came into full view in the light that shone upon and in him as the Father delivered him "out of the power of darkness, and translated [him] into the kingdom of the Son of his love" (Col. 1:13, ASV).

In the experience of this young man is seen the working of which James writes, "Of his own will he brought us forth [gave us birth] by the word of truth" (James 1:18, ASV). James also urged, "Wherefore putting away all filthiness and overflowing of wickedness, receive with meekness the implanted word, which is able to save your souls" (James 1:21, ASV).

The sheer power of the word of God's gospel is significantly displayed in an incident that occurred in Brazil through the reading of the New Testament. No greater illustration of the truth that God's word accomplishes the purpose of God can be imagined.

A Brazilian rancher, far from any direct touch with Christian missionaries, received a copy of a Portuguese New Testament. He could not read, but he had a daughter who could. The father gathered the family together, and his daughter began to read aloud.

Luke wrote in Acts 16:14, ASV, "A certain woman named Lydia . . . heard us: whose heart the Lord opened to give heed unto the things which were spoken by Paul." Even so with this Brazilian rancher. As his daughter read on from the

New Testament, the Lord opened his heart to see and believe what the book said. One by one, his entire family was saved. Also, they invited friends and neighbors to come and hear the book read, and these too received the word unto salvation for their souls.

In all, forty-two persons were saved. After some time the account of the salvation of these forty-two reached the Southern Baptist missionaries in Bello Horizonte. One of them made the long trip to this rancher's home, and after instructing them he baptized them.

There was no preacher—no evangelist—no Sunday School teacher—just the word of God! Here was no church building, architecturally perfect, beautifully furnished, with a built-in atmosphere of worship. In his preaching Paul avoided the preaching of the gospel "in wisdom of words, lest the cross of Christ should be made void" (1 Cor. 1:17, ASV). Perhaps in our preaching we have overemphasized beautiful sanctuaries with stained-glass windows, choirs, and organs, so that the preaching of the cross has been made void.

The author of the Epistle to the Hebrews says in 4:12, RSV, "For the word of God is living and active, sharper than any two-edged sword, piercing to the division of soul and spirit, of joints and marrow, and discerning the thoughts and intentions of the heart."

Not only does the Bible prove to be God's means for the salvation of the souls of men, but it is the chief nourisher in their growth as Christians. This is one of the superlative facts set forth in the famous Romans 12:1-2 passage (RSV). First we are told to present our bodies as a "living sacrifice, holy and acceptable to God, which is your spiritual worship." That would seem to be sufficient. But there's more. "Do not be conformed to this world." "This world" is not God's pattern for Christian character. But there is still more—"but be transformed by the renewal of your mind." The "renewal of your mind" is achieved through the prayerful, spiritual reading of the Bible. Such reading focuses our minds on Christ.

"But we all, with unveiled face beholding as in a mirror the glory of the Lord, are transformed into the same image from glory to glory, even as from the Lord the Spirit" (2 Cor. 3:18, ASV).

I have narrated the salvation "by the word" experience in two situations. Now consider this experience of a young man, a "doubting Christian." He had completed his junior year in the University of Virginia. In his classes he had raised questions of doubt and created a lot of confusion and concern. With other students from his university, he came to a Christian student assembly. I was one of the leaders. My son, Edgar, also a university junior, visited this fellow student and got his consent to come to my room and talk to me. The Holy Spirit really took over that day in our relationship and in the remaining days.

I began, "They tell me you have a lot of questions and doubts."

"Yes, I have."

"Tell me about them."

Then he poured out the whole story of "what I do not believe," especially the errors and myths of the Old Testament.

When he was through, after more than twenty minutes of uninterrupted talk, I said, "You have told me what you don't believe. Surely you believe something. Tell me what you believe."

He was startled by this approach. I waited in silence as he thought. At last he said, "I believe that Jesus Christ is the best man who ever lived."

I wrote it down and read it back to him: "I believe that Jesus Christ is the best man who ever lived."

I believe much more than that about Jesus, but we could start there. Then I asked, "Why do you believe that?"

After about a minute he replied, "Because the people who really follow him are the best people in the world."

I wrote it down and read it to him, and asked, "Do you really believe that?" And he said, "Yes, I do."

I asked, "What else do you believe?" This time his answer came quickly and with conviction. "I believe I ought to do what Jesus says to do."

This caught me by surprise. But the Holy Spirit was presiding that day; so I said, "Let's see what Jesus said." I opened my New Testament to the Four Gospels and before us was Luke 14:26 (ASV). "If any man cometh unto me, and hateth not his own father, and mother, and wife . . . yea, and his own life also, he cannot be my disciple." I said, "Do you believe you ought to do that?"

He asked, "Did Jesus say that?" I showed him, and he replied, "Then I ought to do it, and I will."

We read another passage or two, and he said, "You know what I am going to do? I am going to read the whole New Testament. But not the Old Testament, it is full of myth."

So I said, "Don't worry about the Old Testament now. Read the New Testament." He answered that he would.

I did not have a prayer mate. So I asked him if he would mind meeting with me at 10:30 each morning for about four or five minutes and he agreed. So we met, and I read Psalm 103. We had a prayer and went our ways. The second morning I read Psalm 51; we had a prayer and went our ways. The third morning I read Isaiah 53. After our prayer he asked, "Where have you been reading?" I said, "In the Old Testament." Then he said, "Do you know what I am going to do? I am going to read the whole Bible through."

One year later I met his sister. She said, "My father and mother charged me to find you and thank you for what you did for their son, my brother. Last year on campus of the University of Virginia, he lived a brilliant Christian life and was a great help to many of his fellow students." Again, hear it, "The Word of God is living and active."

What it has done for others, it will do for you. But not unless you give yourself to it; to read, to trust, to obey.

A Welsh coal miner, not a Christian, became interested in his wife's Bible. Casually he began to read it. Then his interest deepened, and he read on. One night his wife had been asleep for an hour or so. As he read he called, "Wife, wife, wake up! There's a man in this book and I've just found Him."

"The word of God is living and active." Give it a real opportunity to transform you!

Prayer and Bible Reading—Divine Imperatives

Many paths open daily before us. All of them are attractive and offer much of interest and worth. We cannot enter all of them; we must make a choice.

We narrow our choices to those which we think are more important. This does not end our choice making; for among these there are those that are labeled "best," "excellent," or "superlative." These are of such character and value that we seriously impair our spiritual welfare by treating them lightly. By choosing carefully and making the most of them, we assure ourselves of victory.

The paths of Bible reading and prayer are given us to walk by divine imperative.

We do not walk these two paths very far until we discover that they are but one and indivisible.

I want first to emphasize the prayer side of the path.

I offer three reasons in support of the claim that prayer is a divine imperative:

1. *God has commanded his people to pray.*
2. *God desires fellowship with us through prayer.*
3. *God promises everything to those who pray in the name of Jesus.*

There are many statements from the heart of God concerning prayer that are imperative in their nature and meaning.

Biblical Evidence

The Lord said to Jeremiah, "Call unto me, and I will answer thee, and shew thee great and mighty things, which thou knowest not" (Jer. 33:3). This word looses upon us a double sense of urgency. There is in it both a command and a promise.

"Seek ye the Lord while he may be found, call ye upon him while he is near" (Isa. 55:6). This command warns us that we may wait too long to seek the Lord and to call upon him. But "ye shall seek me, and find me, when ye shall search for me with all your heart" (Jer. 29:13). To find him and to know him is the answer we most desire.

"Call upon me in the day of trouble: I will deliver thee, and thou shalt glorify me" (Psalm 50:15). When trouble befalls us, we may be overwhelmed by it. Just to be reminded of this commandment enables one to turn his heart toward God.

In the New Testament, from both Jesus and his apostles, come words that bear the powerful imperative of the commandment. Recognizing Jesus' faithful practice of praying, we realize that anything he says about prayer bears the stamp of urgency. When he says "When ye pray," that is equivalent to "pray ye." His teaching in Matthew 6:5-15 is as near being the central teaching on prayer as anything in the Bible. It, in itself, is in the nature of the imperative.

One of Jesus' commandments is, "Ask, and it shall be given you; seek, and ye shall find; knock, and it shall be opened unto you" (Matt. 7:7). Like so many other commands to pray, linked with this one is the confident promise of answer. In fact, all commands to pray are linked with a promise.

"And he spake a parable unto them to this end, that men ought always to pray, and not to faint" (Luke 18:1). Then Jesus told of a wicked and unrighteous judge who cared not for God or man. A widow sought lawful protection against an adversary. To relieve himself—not to serve justice—he granted her a favorable decision. By contrast, God is righteous and loving. He will answer, although the answer is sometimes delayed. Within this teaching is the imperative urgency of the Lord's command.

"Pray for them which despitefully use you." This must be linked with "love your enemies." The two, no doubt, go together; for if one will truly pray for his enemies, he has already expressed one of the best proofs of love. He is becoming like his Lord, who prayed on the cross, "Father, forgive them."

Look at one or two words from the apostle Paul. "Pray without ceasing" (1 Thess. 5:17). "Continue steadfastly in prayer" (Col. 4:2, RSV). Many times he must have encouraged and urged upon his churches and their members the great necessity to pray.

To Timothy he wrote, "I exhort therefore, that, first of all, supplications, prayers, intercessions, and giving of thanks, be made for all men. . . . This is good and acceptable in the sight of God our Savior; who will have all men to be saved, and to come unto the knowledge of the truth. . . . I will therefore that men pray everywhere, lifting up holy hands, without wrath and doubting" (1 Tim. 2:1-8).

What could be more imperative than these words of the apostle? He plainly said that God wants all men to be saved and to come to the knowledge of the truth, and that the success of God's will toward the reaching of lost men with the gospel message is conditioned on the imperative that "men pray everywhere." Compassion for lost men deepens the urgency of these powerful words of Paul.

Failure is tragic sin. "To him therefore that knoweth to do good, and doeth it not, to him it is sin" (James 4:17).

Fellowship with God

Prayer, in the second place, is a divine imperative because God desires fellowship with his redeemed children. When we begin to try to lift this thought, we stagger beneath its great weight.

God, the Eternal One; God, the Majestic One; God, the Infinite Father desires fellowship with those who have been purchased by the blood of his Son.

A king demands and exacts obedience. A president of a republic requires allegiance. The head of a great corporation demands results. None of these seek human fellowship with those whom they govern.

But God seeks fellowship with the least of his blood-bought children. In so doing he lifts us from our low earthly plane to "heavenly places in Christ."

Throughout the Bible we see God seeking fellowship of men. When they go their rebellious ways and break the fellowship, he seeks them out and mends it.

In the Garden of Eden there was unbroken fellowship and man was not afraid; but when Adam exalted himself and chose his own way, he lost fellowship with God and was afraid.

Then there was Enoch. Of him it is written, "And Enoch walked with God: and he was not; for God took him" (Gen. 5:24). One can easily imagine that these walks with God were very important, both to God and to Enoch. And especially was this an imperative with Enoch, that he not miss his appointment with God.

Then, when "the earth also was corrupt before God, and the earth was filled with violence" (Gen. 6:11), God had a man ready. He had had fellowship with this man a long time. Now when it became necessary to destroy mankind because of his corruption and violence, God had Noah ready to be the preacher of redemption. God knew that man because he had had fellowship with him.

God informed him and charged him what to do. Noah was to build the ark for deliverance, then to preach safety and salvation in the ark for those who believed. He built on and on and continued to preach. None of those who heard him were converted; at least there are no conversions recorded. Noah must have felt great discouragement. In such times he turned to the Lord. This divine fellowship sustained him through 120 years, and Noah never lost sight of the imperative necessity of prayer.

A beautiful expression of the fact that prayer is a divine imperative is manifested in the fellowship which Abraham had with the Lord. From Ur of Chaldees to the time of the offering up of Isaac, the Lord appeared to Abraham between nine and twelve times. This could have been over a stretch of fifty years, but who would say that he did not have deep fellowship with God in between those appearances?

Then there was Moses. His parents implanted a deep, abiding faith in the heart of that child. God knew what and how the boy was to serve in years to come, and he watched over Moses. "By faith Moses, when he was come to years, refused to be called the son of Pharaoh's daughter" (Heb. 11:24). Even in the Egyptian palace Moses knew that prayer was his personal imperative if he was to maintain fellowship with God; and all the years proved it. His last forty years are a telecast in divine colors.

God sought out many other men, among whom were Joshua, Gideon, David, Isaiah, Amos, Jeremiah, and the other prophets. But fellowship with the Lord was not confined to those men who were special servants. Many of the common people must have known communion. The fellowship of God was higher than earthly values, and they knew that the gateway into that fellowship was prayer.

But the full manifestation of God's desire for our fellowship is seen in the coming of his Son, himself God. Jesus Christ both showed and taught how imperative it is that men pray always.

Since God desires our fellowship, it is unquestionably urgent that we seek him in prayer. Through Amos he said, "Seek ye me, and ye shall live" (Amos 5:4). And we must answer, "Thy face, Lord, will I seek." Our fellowship with God is expressed in our hearts' worship of him, and our hearts' worship of God is all-important to growth in Christlikeness and service in his name.

"We are laborers together with God"; not laborers together with each other but with God. What a fellowship in service we have! Everyone who desires to succeed in the Lord's work knows how urgent prayer is as a divine imperative because of what God promises to do for those who pray. Whenever such a word as "whatsoever ye shall ask in my name, that will I do, that the Father may be glorified in the Son" (John 14:13) comes to a child of God, he is made to stop and realize that here is something divinely extraordinary.

And what shall we think of this word of Jesus: "And all things, whatsoever ye shall ask in prayer, believing, ye shall receive" (Matt. 21:22)? What will we *do* with such a generous promise?

God Promises All

As we consider Jesus' statements, we discover that prayer is a great imperative beyond the commandment. To many persons this imperative is more compelling than that of God's seeking our fellowship. We are made to face the poverty of prayerlessness set over against the abundance that God offers to him who prays in faith and in the name of Jesus. The abundance of God is conditioned by our surrender to the name and to its complete control of our lives.

If I am to do God's work, I need God's equipment. I need God's wisdom and God's power. God comes to me on the pavement of my prayers to make me able for his appointed tasks.

In our world men build great buildings, great dams across great rivers, great multiple-lane highways. To do these super-human tasks, they create and perfect amazing machinery. With these machines and with skilled men, plus excellent materials and methods, they erect in months what our fathers, a half-century ago, would have said could not be done at all.

No builder ever faces such difficulties as those which face the servants of God. There are no machines, no man-made methods that can perform God's work. But God promises all that is needed.

Jesus gave us the work to be done in the Great Commission. He declared, "All power is given unto me in heaven and in earth. Go ye therefore, and teach all nations . . . and, lo, I am with you" (Matt. 28:18-20).

For more than nineteen centuries Christians have gone forth on this mission. Their zeal and their obedience, as well as their success, have been hot and cold, so that even now hardly a fourth of the world's population can be reckoned as much more than nominally Christian.

Other seemingly insurmountable obstacles confront us. One is the population growth of the unbelieving. The unbelievers are increasing faster than we can make believers. The number of missionaries increases, but the population grows much faster.

The nationalistic religions have awakened and are bestirring themselves through their national ambitions. They have set themselves in opposition to Christianity. The progress of Christ's kingdom has been slowed.

Political ideologies have closed the doors of great nations that formerly were wide open. And in many of these countries where the doors are open, we still have no missionaries.

Our own nation is obsessed with the problem, not only of maintaining a high level of prosperity, but of expanding it. Men are so consumed in the pursuit of greater material advancement that their minds are dead to spiritual approaches.

Our churches have become highly organized and efficient. The preacher and his staff are looked upon as promoters and administrators. We seem able to keep the wheels turning, but we scarcely move from where we are. We reach the people enrolled in our Sunday Schools, but not beyond that.

In the face of these and many more problems, we have grown problem-conscious. We have lost consciousness of divine power. If we will only believe God and make ourselves fully available to him through prayer, we will make progress in performing our world mission. Otherwise, it is an impossible and all but futile undertaking.

The "all power" that is given to Jesus is his to give to us

when we learn what it means to pray in his name. He said, "I am the vine, ye are the branches: he that abideth in me, and I in him, the same bringeth forth much fruit: for without me ye can do nothing" (John 15:5). He also said, "If ye abide in me, and my words abide in you, ye shall ask what ye will, and it shall be done unto you" (John 15:7).

God sets before us the imperative to pray, to pray without ceasing. To pray and not give up! To obey is ours. If we comply with his will, we shall find ourselves enabled beyond our highest hopes. If we refuse to obey our Heavenly Father, in performing his imperative, we sentence ourselves to weakness, fruitlessness, and failure.

"It is God which worketh in you both to will and to do of his good pleasure" (Phil. 2:13).

Along with the imperative of prayer goes the imperative of Bible reading.

At one time in history when Bibles were few, people went to a church where a Bible was chained to a pulpit to hear it read. The reason Bibles were scarce in those days was that printing was a new and long process; Bibles were expensive and most people could not afford one; and not many people had learned to read. These people are to be commended for their persistence in hearing the Word despite obstacles. We are impressed and quick with praise for these people.

But could it be that they were about the same minority of that day's Christians as the proportional minority of all times who read the Bible? The tragedy that exists about the Bible is the fewness of prayerful believing readers in comparison with the number of those who possess it.

Statistics released to the public in April, 1974, indicated that 45 per cent of American Protestants attend services on Sunday. Out of 1,000 members 450 attend. Bible reading and prayer have always been regarded as the great reservoir of the church's spiritual power. Without spiritual power the church is just another fraternal lodge. Spiritual motivation for attending church services in order to worship God is lacking.

A member of a church of the New Testament type must be vibrant with the life of Christ, his Savior. That life is eternal; it is the life of the individual Christian which each receives in the experience of being born from above. And Jesus declared that he must be lifted up, that is, die on the cross, "that whosoever believeth in him should not perish, but have eternal life'' (John 3:15). Eternal life within is the new birth by the Spirit.

Somehow, for many people, the phrase "Bible reading" seems to imply careless or formal, shallow reading that is mostly ritual and imparts almost nothing of spiritual blessing. There is considerable truth to this notion. Let us therefore say, "prayer-read" the Bible.

Peter wrote in 1 Peter 1:23 (AV), "Being born again, not of corruptible seed, but of incorruptible, by the word of God" thus saying that the word of God, the gospel, gives eternal life to a person who "was dead in sin." This is the miracle of grace. This redemptive work is the result of the immeasurable greatness of his power that raised Jesus from the dead (Eph. 1:19-20, RSV). And that power works unceasingly in the believer in Christ through the prayer-reading of the Word.

As we read the Bible, we need the revealing, teaching work of the Holy Spirit, who dwells in us. He responds to our request, "Open my eyes, that I may see." This is what it means to "prayer-read," and it is a richly fruitful practice. Through our prayer-reading of the Bible and our Bible-inspired praying, the Holy Spirit nurtures and cultivates our eternal life by his presence and power.

The neglect of this prayer-reading of the Bible has serious results for the Christian. In Proverbs we read, "He who despises the word brings destruction on himself" (Prov. 13:13, RSV). To "despise" is to consider a thing as worthless. To fail or to refuse to read the Bible prayerfully is to despise it. And one who despises to read the Bible pulls his own house down upon himself.

The other half of the verse reads, "But he who respects the commandment will be rewarded" (RSV). Then there is Proverbs 28:9 (RSV), "If one turns away his ear from hearing the law, even his prayer is an abomination." Why should his prayer be an abomination? One reason is that God has given the answers to most prayers in various passages of the Bible. If a man despises these answers, and seeks for others outside the Bible, his prayer amounts to rebellion and is abominable to God. Compliance and obedience to God's will in the Scriptures make prayer a fragrant incense rising up to God.

There are several phrases or names that pertain to the Bible, especially the Old Testament. Many of them, perhaps all, are found in Psalm 119. To illustrate—"the law of the

Lord," "thy word," "thy precepts," "thy statutes," "thy commandments," and others. Certainly for many centuries Old Testaments were not common among the people, and not for centuries would the whole Bible be possessed by many.

But all that is changed now. There are today great Bible societies dedicated to the task of spreading the Scriptures all over the world. Availability of the Bible is hardly the problem of the church membership except in mission lands.

For us the problem is disciplining ourselves to read the Bible we possess. The problem, really, is a lack of incentive within us. Incentive plus self-discipline will achieve almost any purpose. I heard a Sunday School worker say, "A definite aim, with prayer and personal work, will accomplish anything." Apply this truth to Bible reading, and it will accomplish the purposed end.

But why this emphasis upon Bible reading, prayer-reading the Bible? Many sermons are preached to the end that we "ought always to pray"; but who ever gives an entire sermon to the necessity, the blessings, and the power of Bible reading? I would like to state some motivating reasons why the Christian should seek to master the Bible. In the days of my "Arabia" this became my superlative goal. As others might labor to acquire a master's degree in other fields, so I would labor to get such a degree before God by intense, private personal effort.

I soon discovered I could not master the Bible.[1] I was made to see that the Bible is the Master Book. As Jesus Christ is to all mankind, so is the Bible in relation to all books. Like a master key in a great hotel, so is the Bible among all books. Then I saw that this Master Book is the Book of the Masters, the high and lowly among men who have mastered life and have made the Bible their constant companion. Then a third truth emerged; that is, if you will give it the continuing opportunity, it will master you. As Paul wrote, "You will be transformed by beholding the glory of the Lord."

After more than fifty years, during which I have read the Bible through more than two times every year, and have maintained an equally consistent prayer activity, I say this:

If I had to choose between Bible reading and prayer, I would choose Bible reading. Why? Because it is more important to me to hear what God has to say to me from the Bible, than it is for him to hear what I have to say to him. But I do

---

[1] He usually added: "It mastered me!" (Note: LeRoy Ford)

not have to make that choice. To me they are indivisible. They are like the two wings of an airplane. The plane needs both wings to fulfill its purpose of existence. God's people need both Bible reading and prayer to accomplish God's appointed mission.

Also, the Christian way is a faith way. We are saved by grace through faith. To us Jesus says, "Believe in God, believe also in me" (John 14:1, RSV). In Hebrews 10:38, RSV, "But my righteous one shall live by faith, and if he shrinks back, my soul has no pleasure in him." And Hebrews 11:6, RSV, "Without faith it is impossible to please him." Paul wrote in Galatians 2:20, RSV, "The life I now live in the flesh I live by faith in the Son of God."

From whence does the Christian's faith come? Read Romans 10:17: "So then faith cometh by hearing, and hearing by the Word of God." Other versions vary somewhat, but all agree that faith comes by hearing God's message in the Bible.

You can have a hearsay faith—what others tell you that they have experienced. Or you can have a firsthand experience, your very own experience by reading God's Book. One who faithfully, prayerfully reads the whole Bible will possess a faith that pulsates with life of Christ, the very life of God. Out of such reading, prayer-reading, comes the gift of promises for all the problems and perplexities of our daily living.

David said, "Thou preparest a table before me." On that table prepared by the Lord and ready for our use, are almost innumerable promises. No unusual experience is necessary. If we hunger and thirst after God, our souls are satisfied there at the table as we partake. We take these promises as our own, live by them in faith, and victory blesses us. But occasionally we seem to need a special word from the Lord, and he graciously gives it.

I was asked to present a series of eight messages on "Bible reading, prayer, and promises" to a group of some six hundred Christian denominational leaders. As I considered undertaking to speak to those whom I thought of as "the great ones," I became afraid. Out of my regular through-the-Bible reading, God gave me the promise, "Men of stature, shall come over unto thee, and they shall be thine" (Isa. 45:14, ASV). "Out of context," some will say. But I have learned that God is not a prisoner in a dark cell of context. This line was divine assurance, and it became victorious conviction. I didn't go searching for a promise. I was not even looking for one. God graciously gave it as I prayerfully

31

read his Book. This is one of the abiding joys of such reading.

If you would know God more and more, and if you would experience what the prohpet says, "Let us know, let us follow on to know" the Lord (Hos. 6:3, ASV), you must live with that God in his Book. Thus you will get the answer to your prayer, "Hallowed be thy name."

Also if you would have an abiding, living walk with Jesus Christ, our Lord, you will experience fulness and power by daily walking with him in the written Word. And if you desire to be filled with, and to be empowered for service by, the Holy Spirit, you can enter a growing and ever enriching experience with him as you faithfully, continually, and repeatedly read the Bible through year by year.

The apostle Paul wrote, Romans 12:2, RSV, "Do not be conformed to this world but be transformed by the renewal of your mind, that you may prove what is the will of God, what is good and acceptable and perfect." And that you "the man of God may be complete, equipped for every good work." (2 Tim. 3:17, RSV).

Bible reading joined with prayer provides life's most rewarding fruits. The Bible is the living Word of the living God. To discover this truth is a rare and rich experience. But you only can make this discovery for yourself.

What Is Prayer?

All that needs to be spoken or written about prayer is in the Bible.

God's Book is indispensable. It speaks plainly about prayer and about praying men. It relates their history. It gives the results of their prayers. Many times these results are so magnificent that we are stunned as we think of what God was able to do because men prayed.

There is no theorizing about prayer in the Bible. There are no sermons about prayer in the Bible, and there is no definition of prayer in the Bible. Praying is assumed as one thing that men must do. There are invitations and exhortations to pray. There are commands from God to pray. The Bible is permeated by prayer.

Three things about prayer are set up in the Bible. Prayer is our approach to God. Prayer is God's approach to us. Prayer is receiving from God what he has inspired us to ask.

James tells us, "Draw nigh to God" (4:8). When we turn our thoughts toward him, whether we kneel or sit or walk or ride, we are drawing nigh to God. Yet, too often praying is mechanical. Prayer is more than duty and more than mere practice. Sometimes people think of it as their spiritual calisthenics, their sitting-up exercises to keep their hearts in trim before God. But a great fact about prayer that we need to consider is that we are approaching the eternal God.

Moses went up into the mountain to God. He did not go up in the mountain just to carry out a religious function, but to meet Jehovah, the God who had called him and with whom he had walked through the days of his banishment in Horeb. God was there, and Moses went to approach him.

In Exodus 33 a tent of meeting is spoken about, and we are told that Moses set this tent of meeting outside the camp. This was not the tabernacle because it was set in the midst of the camp with the tribes on every side. Moses' tent was outside the camp. There he met God.

Our prayer place is our meeting tent, and we should go there often. The Lord said to Jeremiah (29:12-13), "Then shall ye call upon me, and ye shall go and pray unto me, and I will hearken unto you. And ye shall seek me, and find me when ye shall search for me with all your heart." Jeremiah knew that prayer meant approaching the Lord, and he practiced it.

Jesus taught that prayer is going to God. He did this by word and example. He said, "When ye pray, say, Our Father" (Luke 11:2). What more direct and simple statement that prayer is approaching God could be spoken? Every exhortation and command of Jesus to pray is an urge from him to us to go to our Father and kneel and pray before him.

The great apostle Paul said, "Let your requests be made known unto God" (Phil. 4:6). The most poignant need of every one of us who prays is to be aware of God as we come to prayer time.

We approach God to give him our thanks, and this should be sincere and from the heart. We approach God in order to worship him. We approach God to ask from him the things that we think we need and the things that we know he wants us to have. We approach God to ask on behalf of others, to seek his will from him in person, to ask that he open the eyes of our hearts, to seek him in his Word.

This is the familiar thing in prayer. When we preach on prayer, when we read about prayer, when we encourage people to pray, the dominant thing in the minds of all concerned is that we are going to God to seek him, to find what he wants us to do, to get things from him for ourselves, for others, for his work, for his glory. In other words, for almost all people prayer is simply going to God, and that ends it.

But that does not end it. That is only a fraction of prayer. There is another side: that prayer is not only our approach to God, but also his approach to us.

Nearly all of our praying is like a one-way telephone conversation. We dial a number; we hear a voice respond on the other end; then, for ten minutes we stand there and pour into the telephone what is on our minds and in our hearts. Before the person on the other end has opportunity to respond, we hang up the phone. The conversation is over. It has not been a conversation at all. It has been an explosion on our part to a person on the other end who did not have opportunity to say one word in return. Most praying is like that. We talk and talk and never wait for God to speak; in fact, we seldom consider whether God has anything to say or not.

We need to remember that God is on the line. The amazing fact is that he is the one who made the call to start with. We would never have approached him had he not called us. Then, and only then, did we turn our minds to talk to him. Is this not what Paul is saying in Romans 8:26-27? "Likewise the Spirit also helpeth our infirmities: for we know not what we should pray for as we ought: but the Spirit himself maketh intercession for us with groanings which cannot be uttered. And he that searcheth the hearts knoweth what is the mind of the Spirit, because he maketh intercession for the saints according to the will of God."

The Old Testament marvelously demonstrates the proposition that prayer is God's approach to us. The first five books of the Bible have 187 chapters. In 139 of those chapters we see God approaching man, and this is the all-important side of prayer; without it there could be no real praying. God came to Adam in the Garden of Eden. God spoke to Cain after he had murdered his brother Abel. God came to Noah, to Abraham. He came to Moses again and again. We are made to see how God came to these persons and how they responded. We are not presented with a picture of men on their knees, but of men listening to the eternal God as he unveiled his will, his mind to them.

A vivid illustration of this is in Exodus 33:17 to 34:8. Moses had implored God to make himself known to him anew, and God said to Moses that there was a place in the rock where he could stand while God passed by. God did pass by, and Moses knew that God once more had renewed within him the controlling, all-consuming vision that his life and work so much needed.

This was true with Joshua, Gideon, Samuel. It was true of Isaiah in that great vision when Isaiah said, "In the year that king Uzziah died I saw also the Lord" (Isa. 6:1). It was true of Jeremiah and Ezekiel and all the prophets. God came to them, and their praying was a response to God's touch upon them.

When we turn to the New Testament, we discover that God has come down to us in human form. Paul expressed this for us vividly in Philippians 2:5-6 when he said, "Have this mind among yourselves, which you have in Christ Jesus, who, though he was in the form of God, did not count equality with God a thing to be grasped, but emptied himself, taking the form of a servant, being born in the likeness of men" (RSV). God came down to us in this marvelous approach to human beings. And because of this approach of God in Christ to us, we in turn are constrained to turn toward God and set before him our petitions. Were this not true, it is possible that we never would approach God. Therefore, we ought to be extremely grateful that our God has come to us.

Here is another way of thinking of God's approach to man: As a servant of the Lord carries the message to a lost man, the Holy Spirit is there with that man, opening his mind, instructing his heart, giving him the conviction that he ought to do something about the message. He opens his heart, and the Lord comes in. At the same time, the Holy Spirit takes up his dwelling in that man. From this time on, every movement to pray is a touch of God's Spirit.

As we pray about God's work and what he wants us to do, it is God who works in us "to will" and "to do for his good pleasure." Plans for the work, ideas for getting it done—all these things are from God. We need to understand this and let God have free access to our hearts, thus acknowledging his coming. Our prayer will then become effective.

George Spurgeon, a man who knew what it was to prevail with God in prayer, said one time, "When God intends great blessings for his people, he sets them to praying." When we are moved to urge and exhort people to pray, let us remember that it is God who is exhorting and urging through us. He is setting us to pray that he may give us great blessing. Recognizing this truth and making it known is a sort of praise that we owe to God. It is praise that will keep us humble and turn us away from the paths of pride that destroy our spirituality.

In the light of this truth that God approaches us, we can use a familiar couplet of verses as a basis of expecting an answer to prayer. Jesus said in Matthew 18:19-20, "That if two of you shall agree on earth as touching any thing that they shall ask, it shall be done for them of my Father which is in heaven." We stop right there, but he didn't leave it there. He said something else that must go with it, or the answer cannot come. "For," said he, "where two or three are gathered together in my name, there am I in the midst of them." When two are in agreement with him, they are in perfect agreement with each other, and the answer is as sure as though it were already here.

This conception that prayer is God's approach to us is a transforming thing. We need to face it constantly as we think about prayer and as we pray.

When we recognize and understand that prayer is God's approach to us and our approach to God, we are in an attitude of heart to understand the third fact, that prayer is receiving. It is not only an act of faith; it is faith in action.

Jesus in Mark 11:24 said, "What things soever ye desire, when ye pray, believe that ye receive them, and ye shall have them." In the original language, the Greek word "receive" is in the aorist tense. That is, it was a thing done at a particular point, not a thing to be done in the future, so that it could properly read, "Believe that ye received them."

This is not the common temper of prayer. Too much praying is asking and then hoping that we are going to get what we have asked for. And halfheartedly, halfway in faith, we wait for an answer that never comes. We didn't expect to get it and had no faith that we had gotten it. But, if you understand that prayer is God's approach to you, and you recognize it as such, and if you have approached God to ask as you have been inspired to do, then you can be confident that the answer has been given. John must have meant this when he wrote in 1 John 5:14–15, "And this is the confidence that we have in him, that, if we ask anything according to his will, he heareth us: And if we know that he hear us, whatsoever we ask, we know that we have the petitions that we desired of him." One who understands this will be obedient to Jesus' injunction not to use "vain repetitions." We are not heard for our much speaking. We are heard because our prayers have been prompted by God himself, and we come in the name and in the will of our Lord Jesus Christ.

There are people who, when they pray, come with a request. They somehow feel that for the first time God is being informed concerning this matter. Really, they are thinking that they will surprise God with what they are about to say. They are sure that God has never thought about this thing before. This kind of praying is not praying at all.

Again, there are people who think that they must come with determination and untiring vigor because they must persuade an unwilling God to do the thing that they are about to ask him. This too is not true. A thing may be slow in coming, but this does not mean that God is unwilling. It may mean that there is still a little thing in our lives that must be moved to make room in order to receive what God has already started on its way.

Prayer is receiving the Lord whom you seek. The Lord said to Jeremiah, "Ye shall seek me, and find me, when ye shall search for me with all your heart" (Jer. 29:13). A knock at my door causes me to open it. I invite the knocker in, and I receive him into my home. Jesus stands at my door every time I go to pray. He knocks; I open and receive him into my life.

Prayer is receiving what God has promised. It is asking, knocking, seeking. But unless we receive (and this is an act of faith on our part), then the asking, knocking, and seeking are in vain. We must learn to look up and with open arms receive what God has promised.

We receive his plans. Ideas come to us as we pray. We write them down, and then we move forward in the performance of these things that we have received.

Perhaps above all, prayer is receiving by letting God carry out the work. Paul said, "It is God which worketh in you both to will and to do of his good pleasure" (Phil. 2:13). We understand this first part better than we do the last. It is God who does the work as well as works into us these ideas, and to receive God's working is a major part of our praying.

Of course, prayer is receiving the gift we requested. If we know it is God's will that we have it and we are assured that it is in his promises, then we can wait because we know it is coming. We have already received it, and in God's time it will be present with us. We no longer continue to ask for it. We simply thank God for it and wait on his goodness. Sometimes we fail to do this, and we start asking again, and we pray ourselves out of faith. We must learn that prayer is receiving the gifts we have asked for.

Prayer is receiving God's promised providence. This is an area that is exceedingly broad. "The Lord is my shepherd; I shall not want" (Psalm 23:1). If this word of God could become the essence of our faith, we would be above all worry and all anxiety. Jesus expands this thought in Matthew 6:25–33 (RSV) where he tells us, "Do not be anxious. . . . Look at the birds . . . your heavenly Father feeds them. . . . Consider the lilies . . . even Solomon . . . was not arrayed like one of these." And then he says, "Seek first his kingdom and his righteousness, and all these things shall be yours as well." Proverbs 3:5 says, "Trust in the Lord with all thine heart." This we need to know and practice because prayer is receiving the providences of God that have already been promised.

In Psalm 81:10 the Lord says, "Open thy mouth wide, and I will fill it." It is said that in ancient days an Oriental monarch, wishing to reward one of his nobles for worthy deeds accomplished, in a very special time would call that man into his presence before all the other nobles. Then he would ask him to open his mouth wide, and tip his head back so that the monarch could fill that man's mouth with precious stones of every kind. That is what our Heavenly Father says to us when we come to pray. "Open your mouth wide in prayer, and I will fill it."

Prayer then is three things: our approach to God; God's approach to us; and our receiving him and all he plans for us through our prayers.

Can God Do It?

In the second month of the second year after the Israelites came out of Egypt, they left Mt. Sinai and journeyed three days toward the Promised Land. During encampment the people murmured concerning the lack of certain kinds of food.

"The anger of the Lord was kindled greatly; Moses also was displeased" (Num. 11:10).

Moses chided the Lord because he had laid upon him the burden of this people, and he asked the Lord, "Whence should I have flesh to give unto all this people? . . . I am not able to bear all this people alone" (Num. 11:13–14).

Moses then asked God to take his life.

The Lord replied that he would give the people flesh to eat and that they should eat not one day, nor two, nor five, nor ten, nor twenty, but a whole month until it became loathsome to them.

"And Moses said, The people, among whom I am, are six hundred thousand footmen; and thou hast said, I will give them flesh, that they may eat a whole month" (Num. 11:21). Moses expressed a very grave doubt as to the ability of God to provide. "And the Lord said unto Moses, Is the Lord's hand waxed short? thou shalt see now whether my word shall come to pass unto thee or not" (Num. 11:23).

The Lord kept his word and brought meat.

Another illustration of the Lord's keeping his word was in the closing days of Nebuchadnezzar's siege of Jerusalem. For forty years Jeremiah had predicted destruction if the people did not return to the Lord. His words were about to see fulfilment. The Babylonian armies had besieged the city for several months; starvation had weakened the Jewish soldiers and people; surrender was imminent.

At that point, the Lord told Jeremiah to buy his uncle's land. Jeremiah remonstrated. He prayed to the Lord, saying that he understood that the Lord was great, that he had made the heavens and the earth, that there was nothing too hard for the Lord, that the Lord was "the Great, the Mighty God, the Lord of hosts . . . great in counsel, and mighty in work" (Jer. 32:18–19).

But the city was surrounded by Babylonians, and the thing that God had instructed Jeremiah to say had come to pass. "And thou hast said unto me, O Lord God, Buy thee the field for money" (Jer. 32:25).

Jeremiah was distressed and perhaps doubtful of this wisdom; but the Lord gave him a good answer: "Behold, I am the Lord, the God of all flesh: is there any thing too hard for me?" (Jer. 32:27).

The Lord went on to tell him that he would deliver this city to the Babylonians and they should destroy it. The children of Judah would be carried away captive. But ultimately he would gather them again and bring them into this land, and they would be God's people, and God would be their God, and fields would be bought, and the land would again prosper.

What Moses and what Jeremiah were thinking was this: "Can God do it?" And this question is pertinent. In fact there never has been, and there never will be, a time when men will not be asking, Can God do it? And they will find their answer in the Lord's question, "Is there anything too hard for the Lord?"

Men say, How could Moses doubt? He had witnessed the mighty acts of God in delivering Israel out of the power of Pharaoh. He had witnessed the great deliverance at the Red Sea and the destruction of Pharaoh's army. God had given Israel water out of the rock. He had given them manna day by day. He had done marvelous things for the people.

And if this were not enough, God had brought Moses up into the mountain and there had revealed himself and had shown him his glory.

But now Moses questioned God's ability to feed this people.

On the other hand, the prophet Jeremiah had not had such a demonstration of miraculous events, but God had been vividly real to Jeremiah. Men might think that Jeremiah's faith should have been stronger.

Every one of us has this same problem. When God's intervention has passed and become a bit dim in our memories and we face difficult tasks, we also find ourselves asking the question, "Can God do it?" It is imperative that

41

we come again and again to the throne of grace and to the Word of God and let our minds be refreshed and reillumined, that we might see and understand the great and glorious way in which God desires to work with us and through us.

Is there anything that God cannot do? We have to answer: "Yes."

He cannot be untrue to himself or to others. It is his very nature to be true to his inmost being.

It is impossible for God to lie, for God is truth.

It is impossible for God to overlook sin. That is, he cannot count it as nought. Sin is a disrupting, destroying, death-dealing force. It is darkness in a kingdom of light, and God cannot tolerate it. Therefore, he cannot overlook it.

God cannot work his works in the midst of unbelief. Jesus could do no mighty works in Nazareth because of the city's unbelief. When God works to achieve things for a man, he makes that man's participation dependent upon the faith of his heart, and if that faith is not there, God's works bypass that man.

As Jesus was hanging on the cross, the scribes and the priests said, "He saved others; himself he cannot save" (Matt. 27:42). As the Son of God and as God the Son, he had come to make things right between God and man. Therefore, because of who he was and what he was to do, he could not save himself.

God cannot be hurried; God cannot be deceived; God is not mocked; God cannot be changed.

God can do all that he has purposed to do; and whatever the purpose of his heart, he will do it in his own time.

God purposed to create a universe, and he did. Within that universe he created man in his image. That man rebelled against God and forced a great chasm between God and himself. God purposed to bridge that chasm so that all who would repent and believe might be saved. They would be brought back within the fellowship of God and to the God-side of the chasm.

God still has his purposes, and God still works all that he purposes.

God has promised that which will make every Christian a remarkable person. Belief that he keeps his word will enable any person to reach into the great treasure house of God's promises and watch God perform what he has promised.

God has promised to the individual who will receive the

Lord Jesus Christ that he shall have a new heart, a new nature, that he shall be a partaker of the divine nature. These are remarkable and miraculous things. Can God make the drunkard sober? Can he make the harlot pure? Can he make the gambler honest? Can he save the lost "good" man? Can he reveal himself to the heart of a little child as well as to that of a grown person? All these things God has done and continues to do. Of these things we are constant witnesses.

Can God keep his promises about prosperity? God has made some straightforward statements to men about this matter.

In the first chapter of Joshua, the Lord charged Joshua to be strong and courageous, to the end that he might observe all the law which Moses, God's servant, had commanded. And then the Lord said, "Turn not from it to the right hand or to the left, that thou mayest prosper whithersoever thou goest" (v. 7).

But the Lord was not through yet. He went on to say, "This book of the law shall not depart out of thy mouth; but thou shalt meditate therein day and night, that thou mayest observe to do according to all that is written therein: for then thou shalt make thy way prosperous and then thou shalt have good success" (v. 8).

In the first psalm we read that the man who meditates on the law of the Lord day and night is like a tree that is planted by streams of water, that bears its fruit abundantly. And that man who thus meditates on the law of the Lord prospers in whatever he does.

Proverbs 3:9-10 says, "Honor the Lord with thy substance, and with the first fruits of all thine increase: So shall thy barns be filled with plenty, and thy presses shall burst out with new wine." This is a promise based on conditions.

In Malachi 3:10 the Lord made promises that would save obedient persons from poverty if they would but fulfil the conditions of the promises. "Bring ye all the tithes into the storehouse, that there may be meat in mine house." This is the condition, that we bring one tenth of our incomes into the house of the Lord, so that there may be ample supply for God's work, locally and around the world.

And God promises that, with the bringing of that one tenth into his house, we will be able to prove him in his promised faithfulness. What does he promise? "I will . . . open you the windows of heaven, and pour you out a blessing, that there shall not be room enough to receive it." That is like saying, "I will open every bank vault and give you free access to all."

That is not all that God says. Israel was a people whose physical welfare depended upon the ground's producing its crops in season. It was also a land that every now and then had an invasion of destroying insects, such as locusts. Also, there would be droughts, and the fruit would not come to ripeness.

But listen to what God says he will do. "I will rebuke the devourer [the locust] for your sakes, and he shall not destroy the fruits of your ground; neither shall your vine cast her fruit before the time in the field, saith the Lord of hosts" (Mal. 3:11).

Some people will say, "You wouldn't want me to tithe in order to prosper, would you?" Of course, the answer to that is no. But I would want them to tithe in order that there might be meat in God's house, and that the gospel might be preached around the world, that they might have faith in the God who makes the promise. The prosperity is his to give and theirs to receive, providing they believe God's word simply and implicitly. That is faith.

If God's children believe that God can do it, surely there is no question in their minds but that he will. Disobedience to this plain command and promise indicates that we have little confidence in the ability of God to perform what he promises.

In the eighth chapter of Deuteronomy, Moses related to the people how the Lord had led them through the wilderness. God clothed them, fed them, and led them all the way. They were to remember and not to say in their hearts: "My power and the might of mine hand hath gotten me this wealth" (v. 17). But they must "remember the Lord thy God: for it is he that giveth thee power to get wealth, that he may establish his covenant" (v. 18). Then God said, "If thou do at all forget the Lord thy God, I testify against you this day that ye shall surely perish" (v. 19). This is prosperity in reverse.

Every person who believes this promise in Malachi discovers a promise-keeping God. The late R. C. Howard, Sr., of Oklahoma City was both a businessman and a pastor, and he was one of the few men successful in both. He was a firm steward of God and a preacher of the tithe as the minimum that God required. He used to close his sermon on tithing by saying, "Any man who will faithfully tithe for one year and who does not prosper, if he will come to me and tell me that he has tithed faithfully and that God has not blessed him, I will pay back every penny that his tithe cost him." After many years of this promise, he said that no one had ever come to claim a repayment.

Yes, God can keep his promise concerning the matter of money. And if we are faithful, it will not take us long to discover that he is doing it. What has been said concerning this particular facet of our lives is true of every other thing that God has intended and promised. He can do it, and he will when our faith meets his conditions.

Frequently God makes known his purpose to a man and then shows that man that he has been chosen to carry out this purpose. God promises great things and declares that his power will enable the man to do the things which God has promised. Then God acts to reveal himself to that man and through that man to all who follow him.

Every work which God has projected, great or small, when completed by his chosen man, has added much to men's knowledge and understanding of God.

The creation of the Messiah-nation, from which was to come God's Anointed Man and Savior of the world, furnished the great divine acts by which our God is known. The Bible is concerned primarily with the beginning, the progress, and the culmination of God's revelation through a chosen people and a chosen man, who became the world's Redeemer.

Within the framework of God's purpose and pattern, a host of men and women were involved. Among these, as the pioneers and forerunners of a long line, were Abraham and his son Isaac and grandson Jacob. God asked Abraham to do the unusual thing: to follow his guidance, to leave his homeland and his kindred, and to go into a distant land which would be shown him. God informed him that there he would see the land which should become the home of a future people whom Abraham would father.

God asked the aging Abraham and the barren Sarah, now too old for such a thing, to expect the birth of a son. Humanly, this was impossible! Abraham and Sarah knew that. But God had spoken, and during the twenty-five years from the time they arrived in the land until its fulfillment in the birth of Isaac, surely they often asked, "Can God really do it?"

That they became impatient and somewhat unbelieving is evident in the Hagar-Ishmael episode. Following the birth of Ishmael, God appeared to Abraham reaffirming his word that Abraham would have a son by Sarah in God's good time. Abraham was to be the father of many nations, but a particular nation would come through Isaac. That nation would spend four hundred years in a strange land as captives and would be oppressed. At the end of those four hundred years, the nation would come out from the strange land and enter this land which had been promised to Abraham.

Before Abraham's children would become a nation in the land of Canaan, God would fill in the pattern with other figures—Isaac, Jacob, Joseph, Moses, Aaron, Joshua, and others—who would do great and miraculous things. The hand of God would be seen revealing that God could do it.

No better illustration of God's guiding providence in fulfilling his purpose is to be found than the life of Joseph. Joseph was despised and hated by his brothers, who plotted to destroy him. When an opportunity came to their hands to make a little money by selling him as a slave, they did just that. These slave traders carried him down into Egypt and sold him into Egyptian bondage.

Possessed by an almost divine sense of righteousness and duty before the Lord, Joseph survived fierce temptations. For his victory he was imprisoned. There he became assistant to the head of the prison, and by a set of humanly unbelievable circumstances, in thirteen years he had become prime minister of Egypt.

Pharaoh was troubled by dreams he did not understand. Joseph interpreted these dreams, saying that God had revealed to Pharaoh that there would be seven years of plenty followed by seven years of drought and famine. Because of his wisdom in such matters, Joseph became the great administrator of Egyptian affairs during this period.

His brothers, knowing nothing of what had happened to Joseph, came to Egypt to buy grain. After their second visit Joseph made himself known to his brothers. "And Joseph said unto his brethren, I am Joseph; doth my father yet live? And his brethren could not answer him; for they were troubled at his presence. And Joseph said unto his brethren, Come near to me, I pray you. And they came near. And he said, I am Joseph your brother, whom ye sold into Egypt. Now therefore be not grieved, nor angry with yourselves, that ye sold me hither: for God did send me before you to preserve life" (Gen. 45:3-5). And thus God again revealed himself, having shown that he could do it.

God's pattern unfolded further with the arrival in Egypt of Jacob and his seventy descendants. The people multiplied. They became one and one-half million persons and found themselves in bondage to the Pharaoh of Egypt. Again, God's hand moved, and he revealed himself in a full manner to Moses. Moses became God's revealing man to Israel and to all mankind. When God laid Moses to rest in his unknown grave, the revelation to Abraham, given four hundred years before, had become a reality. God worked mightily, and Israel came to know him by his marvelous works.

The world knows the true and living God because he demonstrated through the life of this Messiah-nation, through Jesus Christ, and today through his believing people, that he can do it.

God still faces us and offers us the privilege of discovering him in carrying out a specific, assigned task for our encouragement. For the building and strengthening of our faith we have before us in the Bible examples of men who faced the question, "Can God do it?" and who saw him do it.

Could God deliver Israel from an enraged Pharaoh and his army at the Red Sea? They believed themselves hopelessly cut off and ready to be destroyed! They were fearful that all they had passed through would be for nought. But God, by his wind, opened the Red Sea and led Israel across safely. Could God do it? He did.

Could Gideon, God's chosen man, with an army reduced to three hundred, drive out the Midianites from the land? God did it and delivered Israel from their oppressor.

Jerusalem, surrounded by the Assyrian army, taunted by a proud, boastful general, faced imminent destruction. Unless God intervened, all was lost! But there were in Jerusalem a praying king and a praying prophet. They carried their problem to the Lord, and the Lord did a marvelous thing and turned back the invader. Yes, God did it.

Three young men of Israel, on trial for their lives, refused to bow the knee to Nebuchadnezzar's image. Sentenced to be destroyed in the furnace, they declared that God could deliver them if he pleased. There was no question in their minds as to whether God could deliver. The three were cast into the fire, and their faith was justified. God did deliver.

The apostle Paul, God's chief voice in proclaiming the gospel to the Gentile world, had been imprisoned two years in Caesarea. As he sailed to Rome, a great storm overtook the ship. When all hope was gone, Paul stood forth and said to the men on the ship, "Be of good cheer: . . . for there stood by me this night the angel of God, whose I am, and whom I serve, saying, Fear not, Paul; thou must be brought before Caesar: and, lo, God has given thee all them that sail with thee. Wherefore, sirs, be of good cheer: for I believe God, that it shall be even as it was told me" (Acts 27:23-25).

These things were written for our example and for our admonition and for the building of our faith.

It is our glorious privilege to discover and to find God as he reveals himself to us in his working with us and through us. We discover him as he imparts to us some task to perform and with it a word of assurance from his Book. As we stand upon his Word and walk with the Lord in his work, we see God performing what he has said he will do.

Every child of God can discover God at work in at least one place—his own home. Many things beyond the power of human beings are achieved, and only God can do them. Every parent has the glorious work of setting a Christlike example, of being a good teacher, of breathing out an atmosphere of love and grace so that every person who is privileged to grow in that home becomes a work of God's grace.

Can God do it? If God has made the assignment, if you have received his word of assurance, if you commit yourself to him and the leadership of the Holy Spirit, it is a foregone conclusion that God can and will do what he has promised.

For encouragement we can turn to Romans 8:32, "He that spared not his own Son, but delivered him up for us all, how shall he not with him also freely give us all things?"

The Israelites came to Kadesh-Barnea. There they were tested. In fear they refused to go forward under the leadership of Moses into the Promised Land. To Moses God said, "How long will it be ere they believe in me?" (Num. 14:11). In disobedience they turned back, and at God's command they wandered in the wilderness until all who were above twenty years of age, except Joshua and Caleb, had died.

They had been victorious under God's leadership. Had they gone across under the leadership of Moses and had those thirty-nine years in the land with God, it could have made a vast difference in the centuries that followed.

When God calls, we should have but one answer, "Here am I, Lord; send me." God can do it. He specializes in things that seem impossible.

Finding Promises

Throughout this book much has been said about the promises of God which are available to every believer. As I have presented messages in various places on the subjects of "Bible Reading," "Prayer," and "Promises," this question has been asked again and again: *How do you find promises?*

If you read carefully the experiences recorded in the previous chapters of this book, you will discover that God is not confined to any one particular pattern of communicating his will. Yet, warnings, commandments, and promises of comfort, guidance, and blessing are received because of basic attitudes, and practices on the part of concerned Christians.

The fundamental attitude concerns the will of God. "Thy will be done," prayed Jesus (Matt. 6:10). The psalmist wrote, "I delight to do thy will, O my God: yea, thy law is within my heart" (Psalm 40:8).

The proper response on my part and yours is full commitment in heart and deed to the Heavenly Father. We may make what we consider to be a full commitment, but the understanding and experience will deepen greatly as time passes. With every decision we are confronted with the question, "Lord, what will you have me to do?" As for me, there is just one answer—"I delight to do thy will."

The purpose of a promise, then, is to show us God's will or to express God's wishes for our lives. When I find a promise that applies to my own life, it is never intended to produce some selfish result, but to reveal my Heavenly Father's plan for me. So, the basic inner quality of our being must become a sincere purpose and delight to do his will.

The outer, active practice is Bible reading. This is a habit that can be stripped down to a type of legalistic, joyless duty. Or with each reading it can become a delightful experience with our great Teacher, the Holy Spirit (John 14:26). If we have an unsolved problem, we come to our prayer-reading time to receive knowledge of the will of God about our problem. Our business is "to wait on the Lord." Jesus said, "If any man willeth to do his will, he shall know" (John 7:17, ASV); and again, "If ye love me, ye will keep my commandments" (John 14:15, ASV). Obedience to God's will is love: "for this is the love of God, that we keep his commandments" (1 John 5:3, ASV).

Therefore, when the inner quality and character of life are expressed in full obedience working through love, our Bible-reading practice becomes for us the door through which God's promises find us. You don't need to "find a promise." The promise will find you as you read and meditate and pray. The Holy Spirit will speak to your heart as you trust and obey.

If you really delight to do his will, you will not read your own promises into his will. That is, you will not twist his word to fit your own desire. There is a real danger in approaching a problem with one's own mind already determined to follow a certain path. That is not full submission to do God's will, whatever it may be. But what if his purpose is contrary to that which I have already decided?

A young seminarian was praying about getting married to his fiancee. They had already set a date some months in the future, but he wanted to anticipate this date by some six months. He later told of his experience. He was reading through the book of Jeremiah at the time, when suddenly the words of Jeremiah 16:2a spoke to him: "Thou shalt not take thee a wife . . ." That was not what he was looking for!

He confessed that he had been searching and waiting for a "promise" that would confirm his own wishes to set the date forward, which he had already purposed to do. He continued to say that with this experience he was brought to recognize his own lack of submission. Then he accepted this word from the Bible as God's guidance for him. The wedding was performed on the original date.

Another word of warning has to do with the desire in everyone to see some extraordinary sign, even an act of magic. To have God's promises speak to us from the pages of God's Word is very different from the selfish curiosity of some person who simply opens a Bible, closes his eyes, and places his finger on a verse. Someone has told in jest how one person opened to the verse, "And Judas went out and hanged himself." He saw nothing in this, so closed the Bible and turned to another page. This time when he opened his eyes, he was pointing to, "Go and thou do likewise." His magic had not worked!

I mention this simply to say that no immature Christian who is seeking for signs and wonders through magical means will have his needs met in this way. This is to pervert the faith and to change God's Word into a rabbit's foot.

Another problem many people raise is that a promise often seems to be out of context with the rest of the passage.

God is not a prisoner in the cell of context. The accepted and expected context for the worship of God is a church house, plain or ornate, or some beautiful spot in nature. But during my teen-age years the twice-a-day context of my most meaningful worship of God was the barnyard where I milked two cows morning and evening. Milking the cows required no thought; so I was free to pray. Most of the time no other person was there; so I prayed aloud, and the Lord was with me. There was no natural beauty in that barnyard context; but the glory of the Lord often shone within my heart, and I was a better boy because the Lord taught me to pray there.

A good friend of mine, a fellow pastor, wrote to me asking that I join him in prayer for his son. This son had confessed faith in Christ as a youth, had finished college, and was working in the field of journalism.

As I was praying and reading my Bible, I found myself reading Psalm 112:1-2: "Blessed is the man that feareth the Lord, that delighteth greatly in his commandments. His seed shall be mighty upon earth: the generation of the upright shall be blessed."

The rest of the psalm is full of promise. But these two verses were perfect both in the condition and in the promise for my friend. I wrote him asking him to read, pray over, and appropriate this promise, and to stand along with me on this in faith as we prayed for his son.

I was surprised and disappointed when I received his reply. He was twenty years my senior and a man of the Word of God in his preaching. He wrote, "I have never understood promises; and I was taught that I could not take anything out of context." In Psalm 112:1 the context is, "Blessed is the man that feareth the Lord, that delighteth greatly in his commandments." I have never known man or woman of whom those words could be said more truly than about him.

The tragedy in his case was that he had no word from the Lord that enabled him to pray "in faith" for the boy.

No one has ever charged me in my presence that in receiving promises I take them out of context. If they did, I would say, "Yes, once in a while God speaks to me out of a context that does not relate to me. But God is not imprisoned in a dark cell of context. He is free to speak to his children from any context." And he does.

When a pastor seeks to move his people to an enlarged program of work, or a denominational missionary leader strives to arouse the church leaders to increase missionary effort, one of the most natural texts for a sermon is in Isaiah 54:2, RSV: "Enlarge the place of your tent, and let the curtains of your habitations be stretched out; hold not back, lengthen your cords and strengthen your stakes." When we use this passage in such a way, we take it out of context. But no one minds. It is God-given thought for pressing work to its widest extent.

At different times, separated by years, God gave me three promises from this chapter. He gave me Isaiah 54:13, in 1937 for my children: "All thy children shall be taught of the Lord; and great shall be the peace of thy children."

He gave me Isaiah 54:17, in 1939 when a prominent leader expressed hostility because of something I did: "No weapon that is formed against thee shall prosper; and every tongue that shall rise against thee in judgment thou shalt condemn. This is the heritage of the servants of the Lord, and their righteousness is of me."

In 1949, when a small minority objected to one part of the auditorium-building plan, the Lord gave me Isaiah 54:15, ASV: "Behold, they may gather together, but not by me: whosoever shall gather together against thee shall fall because of thee." The marginal reading is "shall fall away to thee." And they did.

Paul wrote very interestingly some words that may deal with the "context theory." In 1 Corinthians 10:1-5, ASV, Paul wrote of God's great leading of Israel out of Egypt. In verse 5, "With most of them God was not well pleased: for they were overthrown in the wilderness." In verse 11, "Now these things happened unto them by way of example; and they were written for our admonition, upon whom the ends of the ages are come." Also, see Romans 15:4: "For whatsoever things were written aforetime were written for our learning, that we through patience and comfort of the scriptures might have hope."

53

It seems that Paul was deeply concerned that the churches should give financial support to those who labored as elders and bishops. He never sought such support for himself, although he insisted that he had the "right" to have it. Instead, he labored with his own hands both for himself and for his companions. As he urged support for church leaders, he appealed to Deuteronomy 25:4: "Thou shalt not muzzle the ox when he treadeth out the corn." What has this to do with preacher's salaries? Paul said, "It is for the oxen God careth, or saith he it assuredly for our sake? Yea, for our sake it was written" (1 Cor. 9:9-10, ASV). How about context here?

When I have had a problem or a decision and I am caught in deep concern as I read my Bible, God speaks. Sometimes—not often—if I were bound to the context notion as my pastor friend, I'd be forced to reject God's plain leadership. That would have led to collapse and failure.

I take comfort from the life of David Livingstone, the great pioneer missionary who opened up much of Africa to the preaching of the gospel. He had determined to set out on a preaching mission. Then word came to him that the natives of that area had just been aroused by slave traders who had killed many and carried off hundreds of others. The natives had vowed to kill any white man who came into their territory.

As Livingstone was praying and meditating (asking God whether he should proceed or not), the promise of Jesus in Matthew 28:20 came to his heart: "And, lo, I am with you alway, even unto the end of the world." Said he, "This is the word of a gentleman of a most strict and sacred order. That is the end of the matter." He went on his way. As he descended the rivers, he met many savage tribes. Not once was he faced with opposition to him or his message. Christ's presence was very real in protecting and blessing.

I believe deeply that the Holy Spirit is committed to teach, to guide, and to lead us by his words of scripture. I have found this way dependable. "Inspired feelings" have led me astray, but not the Bible promises. Therefore, through continuing prayer and through intimate living in the Scriptures, I find the way God would want me to go.

54

Five Special Promises

Before I learned to use the term "promises" concerning particular verses of scripture which were given to me in a time of need, I had already received guidance from the Lord in such verses. I did not know then that promises are a way of life.

In my boyhood God tore me loose from a sin by a verse in Moses' writings that threatened death to one guilty of that sin. When I was twenty, he spoke again from a verse in Acts, assuring me that I would find service and joy in a new situation which I thought could only have dire results for me. As I look back now, I see that this was for me the beginning of walking in the promise path.

In this chapter I am presenting several promise experiences. The first three I have already mentioned briefly, but now I would like to write of them more fully.

In April, 1953, three problems were causing me mental distress. This distress had been gnawing at my comfort and peace of mind for a few weeks.

One concerned the question of my retirement. Within six months I was to be sixty-five years old, retirement age for pastors. Fifteen years prior to this time, the Lord had given me his promise—(Jer. 29:11) about financial supplies in my old age. So this problem did not concern that issue. But should I retire at sixty-five? This was one of my nagging problems in the spring of 1953.

The second problem was a matter before the building committee, which seemed hopelessly divided about where to build a religious education building. We had ground to the west end of our property; there we could build. Some thought "yes" and some "no." This was, in my thought, very serious. Indecisions could disrupt fellowship, and the division could cause delay and bickering.

The third problem was personal. Our church was giving us an all-expenses-paid trip to Rio de Janeiro to visit our missionary son and his family. A dear old lady would say to me, "I am so glad you are getting to go, but I do hope you get back." Fourteen thousand miles of flying seemed certain destruction to her. I thought nothing of her "hoping we'd get back" until she repeated it from time to time. After a while that began to "eat on me."

Then in early April, 1953, our building committee was called for a luncheon meeting. Our agenda was to decide about the location for the building. That morning I knew I must pray for the committee, that we might be united in a decision.

As I kneeled to pray, the Holy Spirit prompted me to reach for my Bible; then he said, "Genesis 28:12." I obeyed and began to read the account of Jacob's dream, a ladder reaching to heaven, the angels going up and down upon it, Jehovah standing at the top. Jehovah identified himself, then spoke to Jacob: "The land whereon thou liest, to thee will I give it."

These words were my answer about retirement. To me they were a plain statement that Jehovah intended me to stay right here "on the land" where I was. I was not expecting this, but it was extremely welcome and appreciated. He kept me "on the land" until I was eighty-one years old. And he kept me physically, mentally, and spiritually fit.

I read on, and verse 14 said, "And thou shalt spread abroad to the west." There was more; "to the east, and to the north, and to the south." And within fifteen years that all would have been done. But that day "to the west" was his directive. All I had to do was to be quiet and see God work. At the meeting a motion was made and seconded and voted unanimously to build "to the west." God did it!

Of course, I read on through the fifteenth verse, "And, behold, I am with thee, and will keep thee in all places whither thou goest, and will bring thee again into this land." That cared for our Brazilian trip.

There, in a few moments of prayer and the reading of four verses, God gave me three promises. That was a rare and glorious hour. So far as I can remember, the Lord has never given me three promises in the same time span from the area of four verses. I have received three promises from a few other chapters, but separated by fairly long intervals of time. Over a period of seventy years with the Bible, God has given me close to one hundred special promises fitted to special needs.

56

On the other hand, He has prepared a "table before me," upon which are "always available promises." When one sits down to a dinner table upon which are all kinds of foods, and the host invites him to "help yourself," he does, choosing what he desires. Just so God has spread his table. Upon that table are his promises about prayer, both from the Old Testament and from the New Testament. They are ours for the receiving.

There are all the strength promises; for example, "The Lord is the strength of my life" (Psalm 27:1); and "As thy days, so shall thy strength be" (Deut. 33:25). There are promises about our economic security, such as Malachi 3:10-11 and Matthew 6:33. There are promises about health—"He restoreth my soul" (Psalm 23:3), and "Who healeth all thy diseases" (Psalm 103:3). And many more. If you read your Bible in the Spirit, he will show them to you on that wonderful table of promises. On that table are promises for every area of your life.

Why then do we expect to receive a special promise for a special need? For one reason, he wants us to have an unshakable certainty and assurance that this particular task is from him and for him.

For example, I was a speaker at a state leadership meeting in December, 1969. I had spoken in the afternoon and evening on "Bible Reading, Prayer, and Promises." At the breakfast table the next morning, two men came to my table. They said, "We prayed early into the morning last night asking God if he would have you preach our July area-wide revival. We believe he wants you."

I replied, "You don't realize what you are asking. I am eighty-one years old, and July is hot. Can I take the heat?" They urged me to pray about it, and I agreed. Through December, January, and February I occasionally prayed about it, but not earnestly. On March 4 I received a letter urging me to come and saying, "All our churches (forty-four of them) are agreed that you should come."

So in the early morning time of March 5, I realized I must find God's thought about this and give my answer. My Bible reading had ended the day before with Judges 17. As I thought about beginning at Judges 18, I thought, "There won't be anything in Judges." Then I thought, "That is a bad attitude," and I asked the Lord to forgive me. I read five verses and the sixth was God's special word to me—"Go in peace. The journey on which you go is under the eye of the Lord" (RSV).

I went, trusting God and the Holy Spirit for everything, and he gave a God-glorifying meeting.

During June and July, 1974, my wife and I had been praying and seeking God's will as to whether we should go to visit our son Edgar and his wife Zelma in Rio de Janeiro. We wanted to go, but did God want us to go? We were approaching the time when a decision must be made. As I read my Bible, God spoke to me from 2 Kings 14:10 (RSV): "Be content with your glory, and stay at home." My first thought was, "That is too plain, Lord." But he did not withdraw it, and conviction came that God had spoken.

Before I retired, most of my decisions had to do with my church work and progress. During these past five years my decisions have been about family and self and work and individual relations. God did not leave me when he led me out of the pastorate. "Draw nigh to God, and he will draw nigh to you" (James 4:8).

This I purpose to do.

God's Promises About Strength

I was scheduled to speak in the four corners of Arkansas on four successive weekends in the autumn of 1972. The specific times were Friday evenings and Saturday forenoons. Then on Saturday I would return to North Little Rock, where I was to preach in two Bible conferences, Sunday through Wednesday.

I was having medical check-ups every three months. Early in August I went to see my doctor. In the course of the examination, he asked, "What are all these meetings in Arkansas?" I told him. Then he said, "You are taking on too much. I suggest that you cancel the two Bible conferences in North Little Rock."

I took his advice and did not "inquire of the Lord." I had hardly mailed my letter canceling the meetings before I became terribly distressed. I did not have God's approval, and I felt the Lord's disapproval sharply. Two or three days passed with these cancellations pressing me down. I had been reading 2 Corinthians most of the morning, and as I read I got orders from the Lord. It was in an extremely plain scripture (2 Cor. 8:11)—"Now therefore perform the doing of it; that as there was a readiness to will, so there may be a performance also out of that which ye have." Could anything be plainer?

But I read on to 2 Corinthians 9:8—"And God is able to make all grace abound toward you; that ye, always having all sufficiency in all things, may abound to every good work." This was great!

But as I read on, the promise was completed in 2 Corinthians 12:9—"And he said unto me, My grace is sufficient for thee: for my strength is made perfect in weakness." In these three promises I received orders and a promise of sufficient strength. I renewed my engagements for the two meetings. After I arrived in Arkansas, I received a call for a third Bible conference, which I accepted.

A few days after I returned home, I had another checkup. My doctor's comment was, "You have improved." God always keeps his promises.

Health and strength—blessings we don't appreciate until we lose them. Faith in God's promises about health and strength produce an entrance into us through which his health and strength flow into us. Have you read and appropriated these verses? "A tranquil mind gives life to the flesh, but passion makes the bones rot" (Prov. 14:30, RSV). In the American Standard Version, "passion" is "envy"—jealousy. Any uncontrolled emotion is passion. "A cheerful heart is a good medicine, but a downcast spirit dries up the bones" (Prov. 17:22, RSV).

In every promise there is a condition. In the health and strength promises there are conditions we fulfill when we receive and rest on God's word. Consider this one: "If you will diligently hearken to the voice of the Lord your God, and do that which is right in his eyes, and give heed to his commandments and keep all his statutes, I will put none of the diseases upon you which I put upon the Egyptians; for I am the Lord, your healer" (Ex. 15:26, RSV). The condition is, "Hearken to the voice of the Lord your God." This means obedience to his revealed word as to the *living Lord.*

Israel did not have a heart of disobedience. A redeemed, born-again person does. If he disobeys, it is indifferent ignorance or presumptuous rejection of God's word. God is your healer; obedience is the receiving channel, the channel through which God deals. "Bless the Lord . . . who healeth all thy diseases" (Psalm 103:3). "The Lord is my shepherd . . . He restoreth my soul" (Psalm 23:1-3). The shepherd-healer!

I was the evangelist in a two-week revival in a great rural church. There was a widespread influenza epidemic in the community; so the pastor had doubts about having the meeting. But after much prayer he decided to proceed.

Every day the pastor, the song leader, and I ate dinner in a home where they were either just getting over the flu or just coming down with it. On the fifth afternoon I began to have all the symptons of flu, too. I turned with all my heart to trust in the Lord. He directed me to Psalm 91. From verse 5 through verse 7 he spoke as if present: "Thou shalt not be afraid for the terror by night; nor for the arrow that flieth by day; nor for the pestilence that walketh in darkness; nor for the destruction that wasteth at noonday. A thousand shall fall at thy side, and ten thousand at thy right hand; but it shall not come nigh thee."

There it was—"It shall not come nigh thee." My symptoms disappeared, and the flu did not "come nigh" me.

About two years later, on a Saturday night, my wife had gone to bed with a heavy cold. I was coming down with it, also. As I lay on my bed praying, God put the promise in my heart—"It shall not come nigh thee." Then I prayed, "Lord, my wife and I are one; may I claim this promise for her?" And I did. The next morning neither of us had colds. My wife said, "Dad, something happened to me in the night. I'm well." I knew what had happened, but my emotions surged up, and I could not talk then. Later I told her. I am full of praise to God!

Does this sound strange and incredible? Not to those who walk in obedience to his commandments and rest confidently on his promises.

"I Live By Faith"

January 1, 1903, was a notable day in my life; in fact, it was one of the "decisive" dates in my personal history. I did not know that then, nor did any other person. On that day I did an unglamorous thing: I began to read my Bible through, initiating the performance of a pledge to read it through during the year 1903.

From my present vantage point, more than seventy-one years later, I know in a small measure how importantly great was that day. In his prophecy, chapter 47, Ezekiel described a stream—"Behold, water was issuing from below the threshold of the temple . . . the man measured a thousand cubits, and then led me through the water, and it was ankle-deep. Again he measured a thousand, and led me through the water; and it was knee-deep. Again he measured a thousand, and led me through the water; and it was up to the loins. Again he measured a thousand, and it was a river that I could not pass through" (Ezek. 47:1-6, RSV).

The tiny stream that "issued" from that beginning, January 1, 1903, has become a river as I write, May 17, 1974.

Many things impressed me as I plodded along, finding the material sometimes dull and difficult to my untaught teen-age mind. But there was one passage that became focal to all my succeeding years in walking with God. I quote it from the King James Version, since that was the version I was reading in those years.

Proverbs 2:1-6

1. My son, if thou wilt receive my words, and hide my commandments with thee;

2. So that thou incline thine ear unto wisdom, and apply thine heart to understanding;

3. Yea, if thou criest after knowledge, and liftest up thy voice for understanding;

4. If thou seekest her as silver, and searchest for her as for hid treasures;

5. Then shalt thou understand the fear of the Lord, and find the knowledge of God.

6. For the Lord giveth wisdom: out of his mouth cometh knowledge and understanding.

I may not have understood a great deal of the rich meaning of these verses. But I did grasp the truth that if I fulfilled the conditions, that is, if I looked upon this search as a treasure hunter regards his search for silver and gold, I would receive what God promised.

Years later I discovered that Jeremiah summed up these six verses in one—"And ye shall seek me, and find me, when ye shall search for me with all your heart" (Jer. 29:13). And the apostle Paul gave me a word: "Forgetting the things which are behind, and stretching forward to the things which are before, I press on" (Phil. 3:13-14, ASV).

As little as I understood it as a youth, those words in Proverbs 2:1-6 set in motion the search that does not end this side of heaven. And I am persuaded that it is continued in heaven and will be one of the countless numbers of joys given us there.

In other chapters I have narrated some of my personal experiences in which I was called to exercise faith in the Lord and his leadership through receiving and living by his direction in particular verses. The following pages contain several such promise experiences, setting forth the fact: "I live by faith," a faith rooted in the Scriptures in general and in promises, commands, and exhortations in particular.

"He Wakeneth" (Isa. 50:4-5, ASV)

As problems multiplied in my ministry, I needed more and more prayer. With the increase of the number of problems, the time and times for prayer seemed to diminish. I could not think of a good solution to this time problem. Then, without realizing what was taking place, I began to wake up earlier in the morning to pray and to read my Bible. This became regular, and 5:00 A.M. found me waking and getting up for two hours of undisturbed time to be with God.

Sometimes I felt tired and strengthless. At such times God gave me a spiritual "shot" from Isaiah 40:28-31, ASV: "The everlasting God, the Lord . . . giveth power to the faint; and to them that have no might he increaseth strength . . . they shall walk, and not faint." I was strengthened and refreshed, and I obeyed to pray.

This had gone on for several years when I asked myself, "Why do I wake up so promptly at five o'clock?" I had wondered about this for quite a while; then the answer came from the Book, and again from Isaiah. This is what God gave me: "The Lord Jehovah hath given me the tongue of them that are taught, that I may know how to sustain with words him that is weary: he wakeneth morning by morning, he wakeneth mine ear to hear as they that are taught. The Lord Jehovah hath opened mine ear, and I was not rebellious, neither turned away backward" (Isa. 50:4-5, ASV). For this tender and loving care of the Heavenly Father, I have been, and I am now, unceasingly thankful. My prayer is Psalm 119:133, "Keep steady my steps according to thy promise" (RSV).

Baggage and Health

The Holy Land tour was a most unusual opportunity for my wife and me to visit the lands of the Bible. We expressed excitement and eagerness as the time for going drew near. The travel agency asked for several things. One was that we send a check for baggage and health insurance. I had done all that they had asked, but I believed that "the Lord will keep your going out and your coming in" (Psalm 121:8, RSV). And I did not feel disposed to comply with this request because of my faith in the promise.

Their repeated letters began to "work" on me, and I began to think of the possibility of baggage loss or illness. Thinking like this led me to send a check as requested! I did so with reservations of heart. That letter had hardly gotten out of town until those reservations became deepening convictions that I had sinned against the Lord.

I mailed the check on Thursday afternoon. By night my conscience was burning like a forest fire. Friday, Saturday, and Sunday passed. Monday morning about four o'clock, I could not sleep. I got up and got my Bible and began to read and pray.

I had thought, Why don't I write and cancel that insurance? But fear of what they would think of me, that "foolish preacher," had held me back. I knew they would consider me "strange," etc. As I opened my Bible to read and pray, my starting place was Isaiah 35. At the third verse the Lord began to speak to me: "Strengthen ye the weak hands, and confirm the feeble knees. Say to them that are of a fearful heart, Be strong, fear not: behold, your God will come with vengeance, even God with a recompense; he will come and save you" (Isa. 35:3-4). This verse did the work in me, and I was ready to write and cancel. My daily portion of reading carried me through chapter 51. And there given to me was a word from God for any that might scoff at such dependence upon him. It was direct and plain. "Hearken unto me, ye that know righteousness, the people in whose heart is my law; fear ye not the reproach of men, neither be ye afraid of their revilings" (Isaiah 51:7-8).

I immediately wrote a letter to these men, told them my problem and its answer, and requested that they return my check. I mailed the letter that morning. Before they could have received my letter, I received one from them returning my check with the request that I increase the amount of the check and return it to them. I was extremely glad that my letter had gone before that request came.

Did God care for us? Who can doubt it? We crossed the Atlantic by ocean liner; we flew from London to Cairo, from Cairo to Beirut; we traveled from Beirut to Damascus to Jerusalem by car; by plane to Athens, to Rome, to Zurich; by train to Paris; and by plane to New York and Oklahoma City—thousands of miles, 130 of us, and God gave us good health, and our baggage was always waiting for us. "Jehovah will keep thy going out and thy coming in from this time forth and for evermore" (Psalm 121:8, ASV). Trust him. "To God be the glory."

The Life-preserving Beatitude

"Preacher, I'm not going to die!" These were the words spoken to me by my friend and neighbor, Howard Oliphant, as I entered his hospital room.

Four doctors had been unable to diagnose the cause of his illness, and from all appearances he was about to die. Naturally a certain amount of dread tormented him. He had four lovely children—the youngest of them just past two years of age and he himself just past fifty.

Facing that prospect of death, he had picked up his Bible. Only God could have guided in what occurred during the next few moments. He opened his Bible, and his eye fell upon the first verse of Psalm 41. The first three verses were the voice of God to him:

"Blessed is he that considereth the poor: the Lord will deliver him in time of trouble. The Lord will preserve him and keep him alive; and he shall be blessed upon the earth: and thou wilt not deliver him unto the will of his enemies. The Lord will strengthen him upon the bed of languishing: thou wilt make all his bed in his sickness" (Psalm 41:1-3).

To say the least, these words seemed astonishing to me, and they were.

But that sick man not only saw the promise that he would live; he also had a very solid fulfilment of the condition—"Blessed is he that considereth the poor."

Mr. Oliphant operated a large dairy and ran a milk truck, delivering milk to many customers. On his milk route was a young mother with two children. Her husband had deserted her, leaving her to make a living for herself and her children any way she could.

As Mr. Oliphant left milk on her porch in the early morning one day, she told him, "Mr. Oliphant, I have no way to pay you for the milk. So please don't leave it anymore." But he intended for those children to have milk; so he told her that she did not need to be concerned about paying for it. She demurred, but he continued to leave the milk.

After a while she again told him she couldn't pay and would he please not leave the milk. Then he said to her, "Your children are going to have milk as long as I have it. I am not asking you to pay for it. I am giving it."

This experience was still continuing when he was stricken. Is it any wonder that the words of that psalm caught his attention? "Blessed . . . the Lord will preserve him, and keep him alive."

That took place thirty-one years ago: he was fifty-one then. As I write this, he is eighty-two years old, somewhat crippled but still faithful to the Lord and to the church.

An Ever-present Help

"God is in the midst of her; she shall not be moved: God shall help her, and that right early."

I was awakened in the middle of the night by the words, "God shall help her, and that right early." These words were an answer to a prayer I had been praying fervently for many weeks. And "in the night watches" God gave the answer. After giving thanks, I began to ask myself, "Where are these words?" So I got up and found them in Psalm 46:5, ASV.

We had been praying about a serious personal problem for a long time; but in the weeks before the answer came, we had become more fervently earnest. The whole verse fit so well. The first line, "God is in the midst of her," was true and perfect. She was a dedicated Christian giving all she had to the Lord and his work.

Having received God's answer through this word of scripture, now I must "stand still, and see the salvation of the Lord." I needed no longer to ask, but to "stand on the promises" and watch God work.

And work he did, and "that right early." Many times as I have recalled this experience, my heart's praise has gone up to heaven for the faithfulness of God. All this occurred about twenty years ago.

But there is more. As this woman has had difficult problems arise in her life and work, or in her family, I have returned in God-given faith to this promise, just to see the glory of God as he fulfills his word.

Today I have come again to rest on it for both her and her husband as they make one of the greatest decisions of their lives. But I am confident. God is in them. "God shall help [them], and that right early."

"Praise God from whom all blessings flow."

When Afraid—Trust

"What time I am afraid, I will put my trust in thee" (Psalm 56:3, ASV). This was a memory verse in the Primary Department of our Sunday School more than fifty years ago. It is a great personal avowal that fear shall not conceal trust.

On a Sunday night many years ago, just after we had gotten home from church, a violent thunderstorm moved across our city. The power of the winds tore shingles off the roof, and the rain poured through the ceiling.

My wife and I were extremely busy getting buckets and tubs under the pouring water. We emptied them and again, placing them to fill with the rain pouring in.

We were so busy that we had no time to comfort the children. When the storm had passed, we asked them, "Were you afraid?" The oldest, eleven years old, replied, "Yes, but I remembered my memory verse, 'What time I am afraid, I will put my trust in thee.'"

That storm experience etched this promise deeply in his soul—and not only his, but ours, also.

Paul J—His Promise

"Do you have a promise, Paul?"

"What's a promise?" he asked.

"A promise is a verse or verses from the Bible that confirm or deny a request. It is a 'yes' or 'no' from God expressed in a word of scripture."

Paul was on his way to seminary to study for the ministry. He had graduated from the university in pharmacy, and for seven years had owned and operated a drugstore in a prosperous town.

While in the university he had been a member of a social fraternity and fallen into the power of alcoholic drinking. Of course, as a prescription druggist he had to be extremely careful as to when he drank his liquor. Even so, the people lost confidence in him, and his business began to decline more and more. He had lost about all his customers when a miracle occurred in his life. Under the influence of the Baptist pastor, he rededicated his life and turned to God with all his being.

Paul had been a member of my church as a youth and college student. As sometimes happens, his fraternity became more important than his church. Yet, he always came to church on Sunday mornings with his consecrated Christian mother. This did not change his practice of drinking and becoming intoxicated. Because of the dark background of college life and his past three years of failure in business, his return to the Lord was a great emotional and ethical reversal. It was a moving out of the darkness of sinful living into the light of life as known only by Christians. It affected him deeply; his wife also joined him, but not with the same enthusiasm.

For two or more years after his return to the Lord and the church, he gave generously of his time, abilities, and money. He never refused any request from his pastor. Then it occurred to him that he ought to become a preacher. I do not know

71

the circumstances of that "call" to the gospel ministry. My first knowledge of it was given me that morning in late August as he appeared at my house and announced that he was on his way to enroll in the seminary.

It was then that I asked, "Do you have a promise, Paul?" I urged him the importance of this change in his lifework, and that he should be assured that it was of God. He was not "too old" (less than thirty-five years of age), but somehow I thought he was not on solid ground in his decision. As he departed for Fort Worth, I said, "Paul, get that promise."

Three days later he came back by my house, having enrolled, and he said, "I am all set to go." But I interjected, "Not until you get God's promise." He said, "I'll see what I can do about a promise," and drove on home.

To come by our town was nearly a hundred miles farther than the highway from his town. Even so, about ten days later he drove into my driveway. This time he was pulling a U-haul trailer loaded with furniture. He was moving to the seminary.

I said, "You must have your promise."

"No, I don't know anything about promises. I know what I want to do."

Then I asked, "Where is your wife?"

He said, "She will be there in a few days."

In a few days he was back with that same U-haul trailer, which had never been unloaded. I inquired, "What's happened, Paul?"

In sobs he said, "My wife has sued me for divorce." There was a court order restraining him from trying to communicate with her. He was crushed. After we had prayed and talked, he said, "I am going home and pray and read my Bible until God tells me what to do."

For three days and three nights he prayed. On the morning of the fourth day, he came in his reading to Ecclesiastes 9:7-10, ASV. I write the lines with which God spoke to him: "Go thy way, eat thy bread with joy . . . God hath already accepted thy works. . . . Live joyfully with the wife whom thou lovest all the days of thy life. . . . Whatsoever thy hand findeth to do, do it with thy might." God had spoken. This he now knew.

As he thought, he exclaimed, "But God, I don't have my wife." Again he spent three days and nights in prayer. On the fourth morning he was pondering defying the court order and calling her long distance. As he waited, the phone rang.

His wife, with a broken cry, said, "Paul, may I come home?"

He replied, "I've been praying for days that you would."

Together they entered a life of service with the Lord. They dedicated their business to God. They became tithers, then began to give two-tenths and three-tenths.

One day Paul said to her, "I have been convicted that we ought to close on Sunday."

She answered, "But, Paul, we can't afford to do that; we make more money on Sunday than any other day of the week. We'll fail if we do that."

He said, "But didn't we give this business to God? If he can afford to fail, so can we."

She agreed, and they closed the doors on Sunday. They did not fail, but made more each week after the Sunday closing than they had in the full seven days before. Paul put a placard above the soda fountain that said, "God is practical."

For several years all went gloriously well. Then one night, driving home from a speaking engagement, Paul was killed in a car wreck. Everybody, including me, asked, "But why, God?"

Then I read about a tragic plane crash over the Grand Canyon. A skeptic asked, "Where was God when those planes crashed?" The answer he got was, "In the same place He was when his Son was crucified."

Suffice it to say the testimony of those few years of devoted Christian service was greatly illuminated in that town. Paul may be forgotten, but his influence will live on till Jesus comes. "To God be the glory."

They That Wait for the Lord

Many years ago I knew a fine student couple who had worked together in student work. Often they had met to pray. Theirs was a real friendship.

In their senior year their friendship blossomed into love, and love into engagement. All their friends were pleased and rejoiced with them. They seemed to be so well fitted for each other and for the Lord's work that only great joy could be ahead.

But about a month before graduation, the young lady became possessed with a conviction that she did not love this young man. She admitted that she admired him, respected him, and honored him, but she declared she did not love him. She was not cold nor indifferent in these words, but tender and kind. For him, the whole world turned black. He cried out to the Lord for understanding as to why such a thing had come to pass. Had they not prayed every step of the way? Had they not sought the Lord's leading? And when they finally became engaged, did they not believe that that, too, was of the Lord?

The university year came to an end. With these things in mind, the young man and woman went home to opposite ends of the state.

August came and with it the Assembly at Falls Creek. Each of them came and stayed in our church's cabins. They talked together much, with each other and with me, because I was their pastor. The young woman was unchanged, and so was the young man. He still cried out for light and understanding as to why such a thing had to take place.

One day as he talked with me, I said to him, "You say you have prayed every step of the way, and you feel that the Lord answered your prayers. Did you find a promise from God's Book?" He answered, "No."

Upon my advice he took his Bible and went out into the woods. Two or three hours passed. When he came back his face was at peace, and so was his heart. He had found a verse that gave him comfort. It was Psalm 27:14, "Wait on the Lord: be of good courage, and he shall strengthen thine heart; wait, I say, on the Lord."

That day he believed that the Lord was saying to him, "If you'll just wait awhile, I'll work all this out, and her heart will be toward you once more." That evening he took his clothing and returned home.

He was going to medical school in January and had five months before he was to leave home. He gave himself with complete abandon to the work in his church. Immediately he was made general superintendent of the Sunday School, and under his leadership the work grew vigorously.

About a month after he arrived home, he wrote me a letter saying, "Preacher, I've discovered what wait on the Lord means. It means wait on him like a servant serves his master." With that meaning in mind, he went on to medical school. After several years, when he had completed his internship, he married a wonderful young woman who has been his companion in everything and a great blessing to the kingdom of God through these many years.

The young man was right in his understanding in both directions. First, waiting on the Lord means waiting for him to work his will. Second, waiting on the Lord means serving the Lord as a servant waits on his master. The King James Version in translating these phrases uses the word "on," that is, wait on the Lord. In some instances it speaks of "they that wait upon the Lord"; but later versions speak in this fashion, "wait for the Lord." Are they not both right? When one waits on the Lord in service, he must wait for the Lord in many things. He waits for God's appointment and power, then moves out and waits on God in doing his will.

There are many verses which set forth this great truth of waiting upon, on, or for the Lord. In Psalm 27 David starts out with a strain of triumph and victory. There is no one who can cause him to fear because the Lord is the strength of his life. His enemies stumble and fall. There is no host big enough to make him fear. Even in war he is confident. One thing he desires—that he may be with the Lord all the days of his life. The Lord is with him in times of trouble, and David is victorious.

But a cloud seems to come between him and the Lord in verse 7. His faith seems to hold strong in such expressions as,

"When my father and my mother forsake me, then the Lord will take me up" (v. 10). He praises God for deliverance and says, "I had fainted, unless I had believed to see the goodness of the Lord in the land of the living" (v. 13). Then comes the word from God in verse 14, "Wait on the Lord; be of good courage, and he shall strengthen thine heart: wait, I say, on the Lord."

Psalm 40 begins with these words, "I waited patiently for the Lord; and he inclined unto me, and heard my cry." Psalm 37:7 exhorts, "Rest in the Lord, and wait patiently for him: fret not thyself because of him who prospereth in his way, because of the man who bringeth wicked devices to pass."

Most of the statements, "wait on the Lord," are found in the Psalms, especially those that come from the pen of David. Psalm 62:1-5 says, "Truly my soul waiteth upon God: from him cometh my salvation. . . . My soul, wait thou only upon God; for my expectation is from him."

David is the choicest illustration of waiting on the Lord and for the Lord. He was anointed to be king of Israel at an early age, probably somewhere around twenty years. He was immediately active in the affairs of the government and became a general of the army. He was demoted because the people praised him above Saul. Finally, to save his life, he fled. Several times Saul set out after him with a large armed force.

One night Saul and his men camped in the entrance of a cave. Back farther in the cave were David and some of his men. During the night he came out with one of his men to where Saul was sleeping.

"Then said Abishai to David, God hath delivered thine enemy into thine hand this day: now therefore let me smite him, I pray thee, with the spear even to the earth at once. And David said to Abishai, Destroy him not: for who can stretch forth his hand against the Lord's anointed, and be guiltless? David said furthermore, As the Lord liveth, the Lord shall smite him; or his day shall come to die; or he shall descend into battle, and perish. The Lord forbid that I should stretch forth mine hand against the Lord's anointed" (1 Sam. 26:8-11).

Many of those who have been anointed king have instigated rebellion and overthrown the government, establishing themselves; but David waited on the Lord.

Even after the death of Saul and after Judah had anointed

76

him king, he was content to wait on the Lord for Israel to make him king over the whole nation.

Another choice passage is Isaiah 40:28-31. Isaiah speaks of the power and might of the Creator. He describes God's inexhaustible power and utter inability to become weary. He declares that the Lord gives power to the faint, and to those who have no might he supplies strength. Then he says that even those who are strong (the youths) "shall faint and be weary, and the young men shall utterly fall: But they that wait upon the Lord shall renew their strength; they shall mount up with wings as eagles; they shall run, and not be weary; and they shall walk, and not faint."

These verses supply infinite encouragement to men of finite faith. These words connect us with power that is limitless and eternal and undiminishing; and as we abide in him and wait for him, his power becomes our power.

What do we wait for? We wait for the Lord to show us his plans. That is not man's characteristic frame of mind. But it is the frame of mind that every Christian should cultivate. The fact is that God has a plan. He does not force it upon anyone, but he invites everyone to seek it. His plan is so much greater, so much more complete, than anything we can conceive, that unless we cultivate waiting upon him and for him, we will miss it.

His plan for his children embraces everything that the child of God is concerned with. Nothing is left out. It embraces the child personally; it embraces his family and everyone in it and all that they are to be and do. It embraces the Christian's personal work, whatever his work may be. It embraces his relationship to his church and the work he ought to be doing there.

"My times are in thy hand," said David (Psalm 31:15). We need to see what God's plan is for our character and for our lives.

Waiting for the Lord means waiting for his directions. If we can put missiles into orbit and guide them to distant planets by radio, surely we ought to believe that when God puts us into his work he also can guide us by his power through his Spirit. That does not mean just general guidance stretched out over long years. It means guidance moment by moment, day by day. Therefore, we wait on the Lord for his directions.

Psalm 37:23 says, "The steps of a good man are ordered by

the Lord." This does not say the long journey is ordered by the Lord, although it is; but it does say that every step of the long journey is ordered by the Lord.

Somebody in typing this verse once let a typographical error slip in and wrote, "The *stops* of a good man are ordered by the Lord." This also is true. John Ruskin said, "There is no music in a rest but there is the making of music in it." Our stops as well as our steps are ordered by the Lord.

We wait on the Lord to show us his promise or promises. Many times as we think about a bit of work or a decision we need to make, we weigh every bit of evidence for and against; then we pray and feel some answer in our minds and hearts. We probably could act on that answer, but it might be a faltering step. If we wait prayerfully, God may lay a Scripture verse in our hearts that will confirm the answer. That is called a promise. It is not that we are trying to persuade God to do what we want, but that God is endeavoring to reveal to us what he wants. And by his words he confirms our decision. We need to wait, therefore, for his promise.

We need, also, to wait for his power. This was Jesus' word to his disciples just before he ascended to the Father. He said to them, "Tarry ye in the city of Jerusalem, until ye be endued with power from on high" (Luke 24:49). In Acts 1:4 he commanded "that they should not depart from Jerusalem, but wait for the promise of the Father which, saith he, ye have heard of me."

God spoke a word of power through Zechariah to Zerubbabel, the governor of Jerusalem. The word that God spoke then he still speaks to us. "This is the word of the Lord unto Zerubbabel, saying, Not by might, nor by power, but by my spirit, saith the Lord of hosts" (Zech. 4:6).[1]

Waiting for the Lord to endue us with power is our way of acknowledging to the Lord that without him we have no power, and he honors that kind of waiting.

We wait for the Lord that he may perform his word, and this he says he will do. God said to Ezekiel, "Therefore say unto them, Thus saith the Lord God; There shall none of my words be prolonged any more, but the word which I have spoken shall be done, saith the Lord God" (Ezek. 12:28). These words certainly put strength into our spiritual lives.

If we know what to wait for, the next question is how to wait.

[1]This verse was the hallmark of Preacher Hallock's ministry.

We are to wait patiently. The psalmist wrote, "Rest in the Lord and wait patiently for him. Fret not thyself" (Psalm 37:7). The word "patiently" seems to express qualities inherent in the expressions "rest" and "fret not." Rest in the Lord and do not fret. This command is perhaps one of the most difficult aspects of waiting on the Lord. We are so impatient that we press the Lord for action when he wants us to wait; but some things need time to grow and develop.

A striking illustration of patience is found in the experience of Abraham. God promised him a son by Sarah. Ten years, fifteen years went by; and not until the end of twenty-five years was this promise realized. Twenty-five years Abraham waited patiently for the Lord.

We are to wait faithfully, steadfastly, and not give up. God honors this kind of waiting, too.

We are to wait courageously. He who says it does not require courage to wait has done very little waiting. We need courage in the face of the unbelief of people about us. They look with raised eyebrows, not understanding, and perhaps judging us as lacking good sense because we continue to wait on the Lord to work out the problem.

When we wait in faith and in trust, courage is not too difficult. I think of Paul's word concerning Abraham, "And being not weak in faith, he considered not his own body now dead, when he was about an hundred years old, neither yet the deadness of Sarah's womb: He staggered not at the promise of God through unbelief; but was strong in faith, giving glory to God; and being fully persuaded that, what he had promised, he was able also to perform" (Rom. 4:19-21) This was waiting in faith.

We are to wait in obedience. God's children are a bit short in this matter of obedience. We figure things out in our own way, work them out in our own strength, then wonder why we have problems. When God marks out a plain path, he means for us to walk in the path without questioning and without deviation. King Saul walked the bitter path of disobedience and heard the stern words of Samuel to him, "Hath the Lord as great delight in burnt offerings and sacrifices, as in obeying the voice of the Lord? Behold, to obey is better than sacrifice, and to hearken than the fat of rams. For rebellion is as the sin of witchcraft, and stubbornness is as iniquity and idolatry" (1 Sam. 15:22). The old song says, "Trust and obey, for there's no other way to be happy in Jesus, but to trust and obey."

79

We must wait standing on God's promises! God does give promises to his children. Whether it be a promise that has general significance, or one that has been made to a person specifically, he is to stand on that promise year after year, because all promises have a continual stream of blessing flowing from them and through them.

We need to work while we wait. God makes an assignment, but it is not an isolated assignment. It has its connections before and after. We begin the assignment, and we are to complete it. Sometimes we wonder what the next step will be, but God does not reveal it until we have done what he has assigned. He sent Elijah to the court of Ahab to announce there would be no rain or dew these years except according to Elijah's word. Then the word of the Lord came to Elijah saying, "Get thee hence to the brook Cherith; there I have commanded the ravens to feed you. You can drink from the brook" (cf. 1 Kings 17:3-5). Elijah did not know where he was going until after he performed his mission to Ahab. Therefore, we work and wait, and the waiting is rewarded by the revelation of the next step when the present work is accomplished.

We wait in a spirit of being yielded to God. This is beautifully expressed for us in Psalm 32:8-9, "I will instruct thee and teach thee in the way which thou shalt go: I will guide thee with mine eye. Be ye not as the horse, or as the mule, which has no understanding: whose mouth must be held in with bit and bridle, lest they come near unto thee."

We wait in prayer and Bible reading. These are the doorway and the path by which God comes to us for everything, and by which we then go to him with everything. With open hands and hearts we can receive his mind, his will, his power, but not until we have come to him through his Word and his appointed way of prayer.

We wait in the Holy Spirit. I do not mean by this that we wait for a sudden inrush of the Holy Spirit's presence. We believe that the Scripture teaches that when we were saved and born again, the Holy Spirit came to take up his dwelling in our hearts. Therefore, we wait in quietness and confidence for him to make effective his promises. He is our counselor, our guide, and the source of our power; therefore, we wait for the Holy Spirit.

We should consider some of the blessings that come to

those that wait upon the Lord, or on the Lord, or for the Lord.

First, they shall renew their strength, and with that strength they shall mount up with wings as eagles; they shall run and not be weary; (and the climax) they shall walk and not faint.

There are times when we may mount up like eagles and run with speed, but these are not the usual ways of progress. The practice of walking expresses perhaps better than any other the daily life of God's child. Walking is steady, continuous; and it brings us, not rapidly perhaps, but at last, to the desired thing. This is a great blessing that comes to those who wait for the Lord.

We are told that they who wait for the Lord shall not be ashamed. They shall not be confounded nor confused. When the work is done, there are no regrets and there is no desire to try to do it over another way. We have been assured that this is God's way, and we rest in that confidence. Others do not experience this sense of deep, abiding satisfaction.

In Psalm 40 is a cluster of these blessings. Let us look at them for a moment. David says, "I waited patiently for the Lord" (v. 1). The first blessing is that God inclined unto David and heard his cry. This is a blessing beyond description or evaluation, that the eternal God inclines toward us, listens to us, and hears our cry.

Again, David says, "He brought me up also out of an horrible pit, out of the miry clay" (v. 2). This could, of course, refer to his becoming a child of God, but not necessarily. Many times God's children sidestep after their conversion, as Pilgrim did in *Pilgrim's Progress,* and find themselves in the miry clay or in Doubting Castle. "He brought me up out of an horrible pit."

David said another blessing was that he "set my feet upon the rock, and established my goings" (v. 2). God kept him steady, and he keeps us steady.

He put a new song in David's mouth, a song of joy, a song of victory, even praise to God.

These are the blessings, as David gave them to us, that come from waiting for the Lord.

But there is still another blessing and this is the one that gives us deepest joy and satisfaction. When people see what God has done for us because we wait upon him, David says, "Many shall see it, and fear, and shall trust in the Lord" (v.

3). By what they see in us, they are convinced of the Lord and turn and put their trust also in him.

Out of our waiting upon the Lord, waiting for the Lord, there grows within our hearts a realization of his abiding presence. We become as those who dwell in the secret place of the most High and abide under the shadow of the Almighty. Fellowship with God can be unceasing if we so will it in our hearts. Walking before him, we are waiting for him. He does not fail us, but works his mighty will in us, by us, and through us, to his glory for the ongoing of his kingdom.

"My Times Are in Thy Hand"

Psalm 31 seems to be a record of a time of trouble in the life of King David. He begins with a confident note, "In thee, O Lord, do I put my trust." But his declaration does not rid him of the oppressive feelings which are upon him, and he lifts up his voice in prayer. He pleads for help and then says to God, "Thou art my rock and fortress" (v. 3). And further, "Pull me out of the net that they have laid privily for me: for thou art my strength. Into thine hand I commit my spirit: thou hast redeemed me, O Lord God of truth" (vv. 4-5).

He swings back and forth between confident trust and a doubtful kind of prayer; but he arrives at a solid footing and declares boldly, "But I trusted in thee, O Lord; I said, Thou art my God. My times are in thy hand" (vv. 14-15).

All of us experience this cycle of trouble and trust. Troubles come upon us, and we are discouraged and defeated. Our path is darkened by clouds of doubt. We cry to the Lord in our troubles. We pray fitfully but not trustingly. Unexpectedly the clouds break, and a brilliant shaft of light falls upon us. In that light we rejoice for a moment; but the clouds close in, and again we seem to lose our joy and our trust. Present troubles seem more real than the God who seems to be far off.

Peter had this type of experience one early morning on the Sea of Galilee. Jesus came walking on the sea in the fourth watch of the night. The disciples saw him come and in fear cried out. But he said to them, "It is I, be not afraid."

Peter said, "Lord, if it be thou, bid me come unto thee on the water. And he said, Come" (Matt. 14:28–29).

Peter stepped over the side of the boat onto the water and walked toward Jesus. But the record says that when he saw the boisterous wind and waves, he began to sink. The wind and the waves were more real to Peter than the Lord who was giving him power to walk on the waters. He got his eyes off the Lord and onto his present troubles and began to sink.

So do we. We swing back and forth from confident faith that gives joy and peace to disturbing doubt. Our trust is weakened, and we are unhappy and walk in the shadows.

Psalm 31 well illustrates our confusion. The chapter is a mixture of "I believe" and "O Lord, help me." David received assurance in his heart, then continued to pray and prayed himself out of faith. But in verses 14–15 he arrived at a solid, broad place where he stood still and said, "But I trusted in thee, O Lord: I said, Thou art my God. My times are in thy hand."

"My times are in thy hand!" This is a fact. A fact is something that has actual existence. God is a fact; I am a fact. That my times are in God's hands is a fact, whether I realize and experience it or not. Blessed is the man who discovers this fact and lives in the reality of it from day to day.

This is one of the great teachings of the Scriptures. Jesus imparted this great thought again and again in his teaching and in his own practice.

He practiced it in his replies to Satan in the time of temptation. Satan challenged him to use his divine power for his own ends; but Jesus declared his confidence that God would care for him. "Man shall not live by bread alone, but by every word that proceedeth out of the mouth of God" (Matt. 4:4).

He declared it in his teachings when he pointed to the sparrow and said, "And one of them shall not fall on the ground without your Father" (10:29). Again, he said, "The very hairs of your head are all numbered" (10:30). The Heavenly Father has concern for the very least interest of our lives.

That "my times are in thy hand" is the most solid reality. It is a great rock of divine truth. We can find great encouragement in its shelter, or we can break ourselves against it. The fact stands unmoved, and trusting people discover its value in every experience of life. It is not theory except to the theorizers. To men who walk with God, no fact is more substantial and solid. So come what may, my times are in God's hands. This I know to be a fact. God is trustworthy and dependable; I commit myself to his ways and discover that he has been holding my ways all the time.

Let me illustrate from personal experience. In the summer of 1925 our church excluded a man for heresy and immorality.

This man came to the church and defiantly demanded that we restore him to fellowship and grant him a letter. We refused to do this. He had acted in the same manner in another church. They had given him a letter, and on that letter he had joined our church.

When our church refused his request, he threatened to sue the church. Personally, I did not think that he would create a situation that we could not handle, so I remained calm. Several times he called and made threats.

Then I received a severe jolt. I came home one afternoon, and my wife asked, "Have you seen the evening paper?" I had not; she handed it to me. Spread across the top of the front page in black headlines were these words, "Baptist Pastor Sued for $50,000." This was a totally different matter now. I was being sued and not the church. I was shaken and frightened and I turned to the Lord with strong cryings and perhaps some tears.

After three days of praying as I went about my work, God laid his word in my heart. I had memorized a verse on the day of my eighth birthday. Now the Lord made this my strong tower. It was the word of the Lord in Joshua 1:5, "There shall not any man be able to stand before thee all the days of thy life: as I was with Moses, so I will be with thee: I will not fail thee, nor forsake thee." By this passage God gave me peace. Then he sent two fine attorneys (one a member of my church, the other whom it was later my privilege to lead to the Lord and into our church). We put ourselves in the hands of the Lord, and God gave the victory.

If we do not do this, we continue in distress and agony. God will speak to us and sustain us if we will but let him.

So, I say that this is a fact that becomes real to us as we exercise faith in God. Faith in God may be defined simply as "taking God at his word." In other words, whatever God speaks to our hearts out of the Scriptures, we are to rest upon. We have no other basis of faith. You may look at the stars and believe there is a Creator, but you have nothing to stand upon in such a belief. You may look at a tornado and believe in the might and power of the Creator, but still you have no faith that sustains and helps. But, when you sit down with open heart and listen to God's word, "The Lord is my shepherd; I shall not want," you have something from God, and you begin to exercise faith in God through what he has said.

Now this fact, "My times are in thy hand," is knowable to everyone who exercises faith in God. This fact operates in the spiritual and material worlds, and experience demonstrates its validity.

We have heard it said, "Seeing is believing." If that is true anywhere, it is in the recognition and acceptance of this divine statement, "My times are in thy hand."

On every hand we find people who prove by their works and their character the truth of this glorious statement. They manifest hearts full of peace. Around them is a joyous, radiant atmosphere. They impress us with a sense of God.

In Matthew 6:19-33 Jesus frankly says: Do not lay up treasures for yourself on this earth; make heaven your bank. Don't have a double eye, an eye for God's kingdom and an eye for money. It won't work. What seems light will prove to be darkness. You cannot serve God and money. Then he says: Don't worry about what you wear nor what you drink. Don't worry about food; God takes care of the birds, God clothes the lilies. Seek first his kingdom and his righteousness, and all things will be provided.

This is the meaning of the statement, "My times are in thy hand." Jesus declared that God is a good Father, better than the best earthly father. Believing in God and in his blessed Son, we say amen to what Jesus has said.

Therefore this teaching, "My times are in thy hand," is a fact to be acknowledged, believed, received, walked in, lived, experienced to the utmost by every child of God.

In relation to this fact, faith cannot be overemphasized. We do not associate facts with faith as much as we ought, but each of us is a fact; and every day we manifest our faith in one another. This manifestation of faith proves that we rest faith upon fact and must do so. This matter of our times being in God's hands is a "faith fact."

Every true believer agrees that this is an abiding fact. If it is a fact, it is true. But not every believer rests in this fact, or in God the author of it.

If God is the God that the Bible teaches, then this is a fact that is most real. We do not discover it or come to know it by reason, but by faith. Many things that seem unreasonable are to the man of faith reasonable and sensible.

No man who will not step out upon the promise involved can know and experience the reality of God in this particular relationship. Once we have begun to step, the fact and God himself begin to appear to the mind and heart. Somebody has said that faith is the highest form of knowledge. The man who walks by faith from day to day will earnestly answer, "Amen."

Faith in the heart operates through obedience in works. Every act of obedience opens up further light and knowledge. Isn't this what Jesus meant when he said, "He that willeth to do his will shall know" (cf. John 7:17)? Faith asks us to obey and to move forth under sealed orders. Without obedience to the requirements of faith, the light dies and faith grows dim.

Faith takes God at his word, for faith comes by hearing the Word of God. God's Word is his will, and his will covers all "my times."

I do not have to plan my life. I seek God's plans. A line of a song says, "I place my life in the hands of God." And a line from a chorus says, "I take hands off my life." God has a plan for each of us. God's plan is his will. His will is in his hand, and that means that my times must unfold his will.

Let us deal now with this phrase, "my times." What are my times and yours? They are the little things and the big things that make up our lives from day to day.

First, "my daily routine." From the time I awake in the morning until I close my eyes in sleep at night, the things in these hours make up my times.

I believe that God is concerned about the minutes as well as the days. Therefore, he is concerned that I get up early enough to be alone with him in his Word and in prayer. There has never been a better example of this than our Lord Jesus Christ. Mark 1:35 says, "And in the morning, rising up a great while before day, he went out, and departed into a solitary place, and there prayed." If this part of the day is not in God's hand, then the rest of it may be out of his hand also. Whether it be five o'clock in the morning or eight, one must take time to retire with God for strength, for light, for guidance, and for the sense of his presence.

Another thing that is in God's hands, as well as in mine, is my bodily health and strength. Physical fitness is my concern insofar as I fulfil the conditions which God has laid down for health and strength. When I have fulfilled those conditions, I have placed the matter in God's hands or have recognized that it is there. I myself find great help in Exodus 15:26, "If thou wilt diligently hearken to the voice of the Lord thy God, and wilt do that which is right in his sight, and wilt give ear to his commandments, and keep all his statutes, I will put none of these diseases upon thee, which I have brought upon the Egyptians: for I am the Lord that healeth thee."

According to some interpreters, this last statement, "the Lord that healeth thee," is a compound name of Jehovah— *Jehovah Rapha*—which means "Jehovah the healer."

That means that I can claim for myself Psalm 27:1, "The Lord is . . . the strength of my life." And Psalm 103:5, "Who satisfieth thy mouth with good things; so that thy youth is renewed like the eagle's." Also this word from Isaiah 40:31, "They that wait upon the Lord shall renew their strength."

My work times are in his hand—what I am to do, where I am to do it, how it is to be done, and the power for its accomplishment. All this is in his hand, and confidently I receive it.

My "finance times" are in his hand. I have already indicated the teaching of Jesus in Matthew 6:19–33. The last verse of that passage, "Seek ye first the kingdom of God, and his righteousness; and all these things shall be added unto you," ought to care for every person's heart and mind in relation to his finances. God is concerned about our finances. I am one who receives both the Old and the New Testaments as the Word of God. I find in the Old Testament expressions that indicate that God is deeply concerned about a man's finances. In Deuteronomy 8:18 God says to Moses, "Thou shalt remember the Lord thy God: for it is he that giveth thee power to get wealth, that he may establish his covenant."

Again, in Proverbs 3:9–10, "Honour the Lord with thy substance, and with the firstfruits of all thine increase: so shall thy barns be filled with plenty, and thy presses shall burst out with new wine."

And in no place is God's concern about our personal finances more clearly expressed than in Malachi 3:10–12. Here he is definite: "Bring ye all the tithes into the storehouse, that there may be meat in mine house, and prove me now herewith, saith the Lord of hosts, if I will not open you the windows of heaven, and pour you out a blessing, that there shall not be room enough to receive it." This in itself is an all-sufficient argument and needs no support from any man. God is concerned about my "finance times." If I am obedient to him, I can claim all of his promise concerning his blessings.

Another area of life which we can call "my times" is in

relation to the children whom God has given us. Psalm 127:3 says, "Lo, children are an heritage of the Lord: and the fruit of the womb is his reward. As arrows are in the hand of a mighty man; so are children of the youth. Happy is the man that hath his quiver full of them: they shall not be ashamed, but they shall speak with the enemies in the gate."

Our chief concern as parents is the total welfare of our children. All of us want for them the very best, and all of us want them to be the very best. There are some problems concerning children that we can handle; others are beyond us, and we have to learn to commit ourselves and our children to the Lord in his promise. The promise that has sustained my wife and me in our "times" is Isaiah 54:13, "And all thy children shall be taught of the Lord; and great shall be the peace of thy children." It is the first part of that verse that constitutes the dependence on the Lord that every parent should feel. If we will let him, the Lord will teach where we cannot even draw near. We sing a song, "He has never broken any promise spoken," and I can testify that the Lord has kept his promise in relation to our children and our grandchildren.

As leaders in God's work, we say, "my times"—that is, "my times" as a worker for the Lord—are in God's hands. His work, his mission, his program for every church must be sought out and received. Too much of the work we undertake is originated by ourselves, and having worked out the plans, we bring them and lay them before God and ask him to bless our plans. Should we not rather seek from him what he has planned, and the work he wants us to do? As he reveals it to us, his blessing will accompany it. Such a resting in his planning will soon convince us of the truth of the words of the prophet in Zechariah 4:6, "This is the word of the Lord. . . . Not by might, nor by power, but by my spirit, saith the Lord of hosts."

This fact—"my times are in thy hand"—when believed, received, depended upon, brings blessed results. Psalm 37:5 says, "Commit thy way unto the Lord; trust also in him, and he shall bring it to pass."

Committing our ways to the Lord is recognizing that our times are in his hand. When we live day by day in such a committal, we receive specific blessings that are great and enduring.

One of these blessings is found in that word "peace." Peace is heart rest. It is not the absence of storms and difficulties, trials and heartaches; it is the quietness of the soul in the midst of all these things as it looks upon the face of the Lord and knows that he holds our times.

Another of the blessings is that, created within us, is an artesian fountain of joy springing up continually and flowing out to bless everybody around.

A third blessing is that, in time, we discover that God has enabled us to grow and to develop an overcoming faith—faith that removes mountains and faith that becomes a channel of blessing to the whole world.

We learn to walk firmly and steadily in the Holy Spirit and thereby show forth a quiet, convincing, satisfying testimony to our Heavenly Father's good care of us. This testimony becomes a converting testimony to men who do not know God. David expresses this well in Psalm 40:

I waited patiently for the Lord; and he inclined unto me, and heard my cry. He brought me up also out of an horrible pit, out of the miry clay, and set my feet upon a rock, and established my goings. And he hath put a new song in my mouth, even praise unto our God; many shall see it, and fear, and shall trust in the Lord (vv. 1–3).

When we believe, receive, and live by this truth, "my times are in thy hand," we of necessity live in dependence upon God and receive all of God's blessings.

Buying Cars and Prayer

"Should a man pray about buying a new car?" I heard this question a few days ago. Is God concerned about only what we consider big things? Zechariah 4:10 asks, "For who hath despised the day of small things?"

Our question ought to be, "When is a thing small?" Is the atom small? Split it, and it can create havoc. Countless grass blades make a lawn. Countless rain drops make a shower for the earth; and countless prayers about little things, so-called, produce a nation. "Should a man pray about buying a car?" He'd better.

Years ago I didn't, and my Heavenly Father dealt in love with me. It was extremely painful.

It happened like this. Our car was second-hand when we bought it. Besides that, it had been in a wreck. But it was well repaired. It seemed good enough; and, for what it cost, it probably was. However, a 3500-mile trip to Florida and other trips began to tear it apart. Every time I drove it, I had the urge to buy another. It would have to be a good used car if I did buy. For two or three months I thought about it, and I am sure I prayed about it some.

Then the ideal car was confronted. It was a 1938 Pontiac with an eight-cylinder engine—the dealer's car. He told me he had driven it only twelve hundred miles, and Mr. L. was dependable. He offered it to me at a price I could handle, and he would take my old car as the down-payment. Any businessman in my church would have told me that I'd be foolish not to buy it. The handsome car; the good business deal, and my need all confirmed by decision. Had I not prayed for something like this? Sure I had!

Suddenly, unconsciously at first, I began to shy away from further praying. Why should I pray? Wasn't it a good deal? Wasn't that what I wanted? So I had prayed, "I must make a decision."

I asked my wife to agree with me. She hesitated for awhile

and then said, "You think it is a good deal. What more do you need?"

Then my college student daughter asked, "Daddy, have you a promise?" My reaction was, "Does she have to tell me what to do?"

By now I was possessed by "car-fever," and it was running high. So I bought the car, and it was delivered to me at 5:00 P.M. Through all this I thought I was doing the right thing.

I took the family for a drive, and it was delightful. When we got home, my "car-fever" had gone below normal, and I was in a reaction. But there was nothing I could do at the moment. The youth group from the church was coming in a few moments for a social time, and I was to direct the games.

About 9:00 P.M. I began to wish they would go home— which was altogether different from my usual love for them. By ten o'clock they were gone. The family went to bed, and I got my Bible to read and pray. But I couldn't read. I couldn't pray! This state continued for an hour and a half.

At 11:30 I got down on my knees by my bed and faced it. I had ignored God and the attitude of my wife and daughter. Now I told God I was sorry. I asked for forgiveness. And as I prayed, the fire of hell burned within me.

Time passed, and at 2:15 A.M. God said to me, "Take it back." And at 2:30 I said, "Lord, if you will make Mr. L. willing, I'll take it back." My surrender for the moment was complete. The fire died, and God put me to sleep instantly.

At 6:30 A.M. I awakened. The sun was shining; the glory of the Lord was on the earth; the birds were singing, and I was at peace. Then I thought, "Oh, that was just middle-of-the-night stuff." And quicker than it takes to tell it, that black "stuff" began to roll in on me like a tornado, and I cried, "Lord, I'll take it back."

I called Mr. L. as soon as I could, and asked him to meet me at my church. In fifteen minutes I was telling him the story of the night. He himself is a good Christian man. When I finished, he said, "Of course I'll take it back." He left my old car and drove off in that beautiful car.

I was bruised spiritually. I felt as though I had been beaten mentally and physically. I went up to my study in the church. Lying on the table was a copy of *The Goodspeed New Testament*. A leaf had come out; so I took mucilage and put it back in. Then I looked at that page. I had underscored some lines, and I read, "Whatever anyone may say in the way of worthless arguments to deceive you, these are the things that are bringing God's anger down upon the disobedient. Therefore have nothing to do with them. For once you were sheer darkness, but now, as Christians, you are light itself. You must live like children of light, for light leads to perfect goodness, uprightness, and truth; you must make sure what pleases the Lord."

And from that hour till now, I have tried to be sure as to what pleases the Lord.

In 1950 I thought it was time to trade and buy a new car. As I prayed for a few weeks about it, the Lord made plain to me that before I could talk to the dealer about buying a car, I must talk to him about being a Christian. Mr. P. had been a faithful attender in our services for quite a while. We all assumed that he was not a Christian because he did not belong to the church. So when the Lord made known that I must talk salvation before talking car, I did.

I prayed for at least a week about this assignment. One morning I felt in my soul that the Holy Spirit was leading me to do it then. I went into Mr. P.'s office, and he invited me to be seated across the desk from him.

Without any preliminary remarks I said, "Mr. P., I want to talk to you about being a Christian."

His next words shocked me. He said, "Mr. Hallock, I am a Christian. I was saved at the age of sixteen in a country church revival near Meeker, Oklahoma. I was received for baptism, but, being a country church, they never did baptize me. I am saved and need to join your church and be baptized. And I am planning to do it soon." Then he said, "I haven't always lived a good Christian life, but I know I am saved."

We visited awhile and I encouraged him to act soon. He said, "I will." In a few weeks he did. He is still active.

I came back a week later, clear before the Lord, and bought a car.

The experience concerning the last car we purchased was a matter of prayer and promise. This was the year 1965. I was seventy-seven years old. The Lord had kept me doing full-time work in my pastorate. But the question came, "How long will I be pastor and have adequate income to make monthly car payments?" This was a grave issue at age seventy-seven. After much prayer the Lord gave me an unexcelled answer found in 1 Kings 17:14—"For thus says the Lord the God of Israel, 'The jar of meal shall not be spent, and the cruse of oil shall not fail'" (RSV).

I bear testimony that, as always, through this time, too, God was faithful.

On March 2, 1969, I resigned my pastorate with income greatly reduced. I was not to be without work—but again the question of "ability to pay" intruded in our thoughts about a new car. We prayed not for a new car, but for God's will to be revealed. A few weeks passed and it became clear that I was to do nothing. As I drove into my garage, I said, "Lord Jesus, if you want us to keep this car and make it do for our remaining years, we'll be pleased to do that."

Ten or fifteen days after that, I was in my study at the church visiting with a couple about to leave for service in the United States Navy. Some men filed into the room, about twenty of them. I thought they were there to give this young couple a farewell. Instead I was handed a "Thank you" card with twenty-six names on it. Then they invited us to come out to the street. The leader of the group said to me, "Give me the keys to your Pontiac, and I will give you the keys to that new LeSabre Buick." It was a heavenly surprise, and these men were God's agents.

"The Lord is my shepherd; I shall not want." Great is God's faithfulness.

God guides us in all things if we yield to his will. Not to yield brings failure and pain.

In a college class in Robert Browning's poetry in my senior year I memorized the first stanza of "Rabbi ben Ezra." From it I acquired an inspiring ideal to grow old gracefully. That stanza seemed almost God-inspired. This is the stanza:

Grow old along with me!
The best is yet to be,
The last of life for which the first was made:
Our times are in His hand
Who saith, "A whole I planned,
Youth shows but half; trust God: see all, nor be afraid."

I was still young, and all my life was before me. However, I was mature enough to know that I was on the threshold over which I was about to enter manhood. I did not know it then; but in the course of time, I was made to know that at first you are a "young adult," "the great potential leader."

Then in a flash I was a "middle-aged adult," the mature person. And before I had time to use middle adult potentials to their fulness, I found myself fifty years old.

In a meeting of fellow pastors who were discussing financial retirement security, I heard it said, "when you are fifty years old, nobody wants you." The speaker cited the case of a fifty-year-old pastor who had resigned from his pulpit and had sought in vain for a church that would make him their pastor. Just having had my fiftieth birthday six weeks previously, I was much disturbed by this idea.

What was to be done? I carried this matter in my prayers to the Lord. My committal to him was, "Lord, I'm fifty years old. I am going to let you see what you can do with me from here on." This was just an extension of my relationship with him, but now made more vivid by the declaration, "When you are fifty years old, you are through." But my poem said, "the best is yet to be, the last of life for which the first was made." So I welcomed each new year gladly and looked on toward the next.

When I was eighty-five, my great-grandson, five years old, asked, "Granddad, why are you getting old?" That's a profound question.

I answered, "For the same reason that you are going to be six years old your next birthday."

Yes, the days pass, and new days come. We are young men, and then one day someone asks, "How are you, *Granddad?*" But my heart sings, "The best is yet to be."

If "old age" were just a matter of many years, we might ignore it. The attitude we assume toward these many years, or toward the spot where we are, is what makes "old age" good or bad. Rabbi ben Ezra says, "The best is yet to be." Today better than yesterday? Tomorrow better than today? Is it so? Faith answers, "But I trust in thee, O Lord. I say, 'Thou art my God.' My times are in thy hand" (Psalm 31:14–15a RSV).

"My times are in thy hand." Yes, "the best is yet to be"! It is God who handles our times in his hand, and who plans the whole of life (Phil. 2:13, RSV; Jer. 29:11, RSV). He planned youth as first steps in a life that climbs steadily to the last step, good all the way. God cannot plan it otherwise. "Old age" is that "last of life" for which "the first was made."

Henry Wadsworth Longfellow wrote about the achievements of men who were advanced in years, men of whom we say, they are "old men." But read it:

It is too late. Ah, nothing is too late.
Cato learned Greek at eighty, Sophocles
Wrote his grand "Oedipus" and Simonides
Bore off the prize of verse from his compeers
When each had numbered more than four score years:
And Theophrastus at four score and ten
Had begun his "Characters of Men."
Chaucer, at Woodstock, with the nightingales
At sixty, wrote "The Canterbury Tales."
Goethe, at Weimer, toiling to the last,
Completed "Faust" when eighty years were past.
What then? Shall we sit idly down and say,
"The night has come, it is no longer day"?
For age is opportunity, no less
Than youth itself, though in another dress.
And as the evening twilight fades away,
The sky is filled with stars invisible by day.

God is no respecter of persons, neither racially (Acts 10:34) nor of persons as to age. When he needed a Moses, he did not ask, "How old are you?" But he called the eighty-year-old man and gave him vision and strength to toil on for another forty years. God laid his hand on Joshua, one hundred years old, and gave him ten years of special leadership in which to settle Israel in the Promised Land.

When God needed a prophet to teach Israel, he found Isaiah, still in his twenties. And Jeremiah responded to God's appointment, "a prophet of the nations," with, "Ah, Lord God! Behold, I do not know how to speak for I am only a youth" (Jer. 1:4–8, RSV). But the Lord said, "Do not say, 'I am only a youth.'"

We make much of strongly committed Christian youth. And we should. Old men, strongly committed to Christ, need no plaudits; for they have proved him and know that he alone has the words and power of life. For all men, young and old, the will and purpose of God are of prime importance and concern.

The apostle Paul was about thirty years of age when Jesus presented himself to him on the Damascus road. That day Paul's question was, "What wilt thou have me to do"? That's my daily question and yours, until the Lord calls us home. In youth we seek to know to what work our Heavenly Father would have us give our lives. In old age we are still seeking his will and work for each day. God is no less concerned that we work in his field in old age than he was that we know and do his work through youth and adulthood. For this reason our daily prayer at all times is, "Lord, what wilt thou have me to do?" In his wisdom God calls us to the tasks for which he has qualified us.

Our attitude as men and women of advanced years is one of cheerful compliance and loving obedience as our Father leads. Always, as dedicated servants of the Lord, "Seek ye first the kingdom of God, and his righteousness" has been our unfailing goal. Now, as old age opens up, it is more than ever our goal. For soon we'll pass from the field of seeking to the realm of divine fulfilment.

One of the dreaded specters that blackens the sky of the aging is uselessness. I was well into my eighty-first year when I felt that God was giving me the inner urge to resign my pastorate and retire. For ten months I prayed before my directive came from him. Then when I fully realized that the Lord was in my resignation, I got a feeling of being dropped from an active whirl of work into a vacuum of nothing to do. I did at that moment what I believe everyone ought to do: I bowed my heart before the Lord and said, "Lord, I don't want to be idle. Give me work that I can do."

His answer came quickly, "Launch out into the deep, and let down your nets." I was ready to do that, since it was from him. The next morning I prayed and said, "Lord, it might help to confirm your word, if you would give me a call today." For my own good I wrote that in my book.

During the busy-ness of the day, I forgot about a call. But not God! That night at ten o'clock, a long distance phone call came from a pastor six hundred miles away, telling me that the deacons had just authorized him to call me for an eight-day meeting.

God didn't say to me, "You are too old—you can't do it." No, this was God launching me into his new field of work. And this was before I had presented my resignation.

Five months later I retired. God has kept me busy, happy, and fruitful in his work. That was five years ago. With David I say, "My times are in thy hand," and with Browning I believe,

Our times are in His hand
Who saith, "A whole I planned,
Youth shows but half; trust God!"

Eliphaz, Job's friend, spoke a great word for all the aged when he said to Job, "You shall come to your grave in ripe old age, as a shock of grain comes up to the threshing floor in its season" (Job 5:26). Job was in deep trouble and sorely hurt with sorrow and ill health. Job did not know it then, but for Job, "the best [was] yet to be."

At the last, the Lord spoke revealing himself to Job (chaps. 38–41); Job was humbled and confessed, "I have heard of thee by the hearing of the ear: but now mine eye seeth thee. Wherefore I abhor myself, and repent in dust and ashes" (Job 42:5).

The Lord then appointed Job to the ministry of intercessory prayer. The Lord's wrath was kindled against Job's three friends. And he said to them, "Now therefore take seven bulls and seven rams, and go to my servant Job, and offer up for yourselves a burnt offering; and my servant Job shall pray for you, for I will accept his prayer not to deal with you according to your folly" (Job 42:8, RSV).

This they did. "And the Lord accepted Job's prayer. And the Lord restored the fortunes of Job, when he had prayed for his friends; and the Lord gave Job twice as much as he had before . . . and the Lord blessed the latter days of Job more than his beginning" (Job 42:10, 12, RSV).

At the age of fifty, I met head-on one of the thorniest problems of old age—the problem of financial security. For more than thirty-five years I had read the Bible two to four times each year, and the New Testament much more often. Jesus' teaching concerning the Heavenly Father's concern for his children deeply affected me. He taught us to pray in simplicity and in sincerity, and that "your Father knows." He feeds the birds, he clothes the lilies of the field; so be not anxious about what you will eat or what you will wear. Your Heavenly Father knows about what you need. "Seek ye first the kingdom of God, and his righteousness; and all these things shall be added unto you" (Matt. 6:25–33).

I had read these beautiful things spoken by Jesus, and I believed them. But there is believing—then there is BELIEVING. The remark made by a college girl in prayer meeting opened my eyes. She said, "You adults make me weary. I hear you quoting Jesus' word, 'Seek ye first the kingdom of God!' But I don't see any of you doing it."

That night her remark changed my life, even though I did not know it then. The change was not observed; but had anyone been able to read the prayers of my heart, he might have observed a change toward a more sincere faith in Jesus and his words. I myself was not aware of any change. For thirteen years I had simply prayed over and over, "Lord, help me to seek first your kingdom and your righteousness."

At the end of those thirteen years, I got the answer. Should I accept the preachers' retirement program for my old age, or should I trust Jesus to provide in this promise which he gave in Matthew 6:33? When age sixty-five years with retirement would arrive, what would be my financial dependence, a Scripture promise from Jesus or a denominational program? I was never opposed to that program of my denomination. But I was held by Jesus' promise in a viselike grip. I had read that a belief is what you hold; a conviction is what holds you. I had been given a conviction, an anchor, and it held.

When the moment of decision came, I went to the Lord in prayer. I knew my preacher brethren would consider me foolish, but it was God I must please. With my open Bible on a chair beside me, I knelt and prayed, "Lord, if I ever needed a promise in all my life, I need one tonight." And after awhile I started to get up and read my Bible, waiting on God for a word of guidance.

But He didn't let me get up. He directed my eyes to my open Bible, and there before me I read Jeremiah 29:11 (ASV), "I know the thoughts that I think toward you, saith Jehovah, thoughts of peace, and not of evil, to give you hope in your latter end." That was sufficient! I thanked him and went to bed. God has been faithful. He gave favor with my church that at the age of eighty-one I was enabled to complete forty-six years as their pastor. I take my stand and affirm with Paul, "I believe God, that it shall be even so as it hath been spoken unto me" (Acts 27:25, ASV).

The real key that unlocks the door into God's care lies in the question, "Lord, what wilt thou have me to do"? Consciously or unconsciously we ask that question every day. God, our Father, and Jesus Christ, our Savior, have a thing for us to be and to do every day. If I believe that question and ask it sincerely, I am made to know that my welfare is of prime concern to my Heavenly Father.

Not only is our wealth his care, but also our health. "He restoreth my soul" means he restores my life. He makes me physically well, and living in him keeps me well. "A cheerful spirit is a good medicine."

The Lord said through Isaiah, "Even to old age I am he, and even to hoar hairs will I carry you. I have made, and I will bear; yea, I will carry, and will deliver" (Isa. 46:4, ASV).

And the psalmist wrote (Psalm 92:12–15, ASV):

The righteous shall flourish like the palm-tree:
    He shall grow like a cedar in Lebanon.
They are planted in the house of Jehovah;
    They shall flourish in the courts of our God.
They shall still bring forth fruit in old age;
    They shall be full of sap and green:
To show that Jehovah is upright;
He is my rock, and there is no unrighteous-
ness in him.

We sing the great hymn, "How Firm a Foundation" with more appreciation in old age than in youth. Read these two stanzas,

How firm a foundation, ye saints of the Lord,
Is laid for your faith in His excellent word!
What more can He say than to you He hath said,
To you who for refuge to Jesus have fled?
. . . .
E'en down to old age, all my people shall prove
My sovereign, eternal, unchangeable love!
And when hoary hairs shall their temples
adorn,
Like lambs they shall still in my bosom
be borne.

"My times are in thy hand." "The best is yet to be."

Again hear Longfellow,

What then? Shall we sit idly down and say,
"The night has come, it is no longer day"?
For age is opportunity, no less
Than youth itself, though in another dress.
And as the evening twilight fades away,
The sky is filled with stars invisible by day.
                    I press on!

100

My Stewardship of Pain
March 4, 1976

This is my testimony concerning my illness and the things that God revealed to me concerning it. I present it in the hope that it will be a strengthening challenge to anybody else who may have come into the same situation.

Around the fifth of last June, I was informed by my doctor that a bone scan revealed seven tumors in my bones, all of them malignant, some in my rib cage, and some in the pelvic bone. My doctor found it very difficult to tell me.

I said to my doctor, "Now listen doctor, you and I have talked about this before, and we've got a common understanding that you're not to feel any unusual concern for my welfare or for what happens to me, because God is taking care of me." And I feel that way about it.

Then I said to the doctor, "I would like to tell you of an actual experience that happened a long time ago. When we came to Norman in 1923, there was in the First Baptist Church of Oklahoma City a pastor who later moved to Washington, D.C. to become the pastor of a large church there. Shortly after he became pastor in Washington, it was discovered that he had terminal cancer of a kind that was extremely painful.

One day a pastor friend visited him. During the visit, not knowing what to do, the visiting pastor began to try to sympathize with the man who had the cancer. The sick one answered, "Please, don't try to sympathize with me; I've already tried to be a good steward of everything God has given me. And I want to be a good steward of this pain." I was tremendously impressed at the time by that man's idea that since his suffering was from God, he should bear it as a child of God would—with courage.

That idea lingered deeply in my mind. Soon, other things began to come along in my life that were helpful with the general problem of pain. About 1917, when I was a very young pastor in my first pastorate in Pittsburg, Kansas, I subscribed to the *British Weekly*, a journal published, I believe, in London. On the cover page of one issue was a poem, entitled "Pain's Power." It went something like this:

The cry of man's anguish went up to God,
"Lord, take away pain!
The shadow that darkens the world Thou hast made;
The close coiling chain
That strangles the heart: the burden that weighs
On the wings that would soar—
Lord, take away pain from the world Thou hast made
That it love Thee the more!"

Then answered the Lord to the cry of the world,
"Shall I take away pain,
And with it the power of the soul to endure,
Made strong by the strain?
Shall I take away pity that knits heart to heart,
And sacrifice high?
Will ye lose all your heroes that lift from the fire
White brows to the sky?
Shall I take away love that redeems with a price,
And smiles with its loss?
Can ye spare from your lives that would cling unto mine
The Christ on his cross?"[1]

I memorized that poem then, and it became pretty much the heart of my so-called Christian philosophy about pain. I was a young man; I knew nothing from having experienced any great pain. But I realized that pain was the common experience of men and that I would have to minister to people who had such pain.

Then I remember so well beginning to discover that God's truth from the Bible is not imparted to the heart by seminary teachers. It comes from the Holy Spirit. He takes the truth and lays it in the heart. I had read this Scripture many times, but it had never occurred to me that it had any reference to actual human beings of our time. But Paul said in Romans 5, "We also rejoice in our tribulation." I thought that was a tremendous statement, a statement of courage and faith, and it was extremely expressive of Paul's own life.

Then I began to discover other Scriptures that had to do with pain. I let them begin to take hold of my life. The

---

[1]Author unknown.

Scriptures, especially the New Testament, are full of teachings on the subject. Jesus said, "Blessed are they that are persecuted for righteousness' sake" (Matthew 5:10). What greater statement is there on the blessing of pain than that? And then consider His word in Colossians 1:24: "Now I rejoice in my sufferings for your sake and fill up on my part that which is lacking of the afflictions of Christ in my flesh for His body's sake which is the church." I read a sermon on that text that helped me tremendously to understand that through suffering *for* the gospel and *in* the gospel, we impress people *with* the gospel more than in any other experience.

There are great illustrations in history of people such as Adoniram Judson and his wife and their tremendous suffering in the British-Burma war. They suffered not as Americans nor British nor Burmese, but as Christians. Burma had been closed to the gospel of Christ until after that war, when Judson's sufferings for Burma opened the heart of Burma to the gospel. It is said by missionary authorities that on a percentage basis, more people were converted to Jesus out of Burma than out of any of the other great missionary efforts. Here was an instance of one who was filling up in his body the sufferings of Christ, for the sake of the church and for the sake of the gospel. My knowledge of the suffering and pain problem was deepening, turning into a great asset for the kingdom of God.

About 25 years ago I was impressed afresh with a Scripture that's familiar to everybody in the 21st chapter of John. At the breakfast that morning by the lake, Jesus said to Peter, "Lovest thou me?" Then He said to Peter, "When you were young you girded yourself and went where you would, but when you grow old, another will gird you and they will lead you where you would not go" (John 21:18). And John added this line, "This He spoke indicating by what manner of death he should glorify God" (John 21:19). This line stands out after fifty years of reading it in order to give myself an ideal for the day of my dying when that time should come. I always thought that death should be a God-glorifying thing, not only my death, but also that of others, and that death is really our last great chance of glorifying God. That's where my thinking rested for awhile.

Then one day I realized that death is a wider subject than just a physical thing—I was dying all the time to something. I'd been an avid baseball player; I got out and played hard

103

ball with the young men. When I was 35 years of age, I gave it up. *I died to that type of baseball.* Later on, I died to playing golf because my eyes had become so dim with cataracts that I couldn't see where the balls went, so I had to give it up. *I died to golf.* All these things were a shock, but I was able to give them up in such a manner that God would be glorified by the quiet influence of my sacrifice.

Then things began to happen a little more rapidly. I had my cataracts removed, and before I was through with that experience, *I had given up, or died to driving, my car.* I just turned over the driving to my wife and gave it up.

Other troublesome things since then have come along, and the latest is the bone cancer. The doctor said to me, "Now I want you to give up all this traveling to these various places for preaching." He said, "You can't do it." This was difficult. Traveling to preach had been my life in a way that I can't explain. But he said I must give it up, and *I died to going out to churches and giving my testimony* to the reading of the Bible and the power of prayer and the gift of God's promises.

There have been other experiences, but this kind of dying is, I think, what Jesus meant, and I think this is what He wants us to do. There's not one among us who isn't dying to something that's very real and essential to his life. He has the opportunity to glorify God by the manner in which he dies to that thing.

Now let me put a little different slant on all this. People say, "Well, you don't think that God sent you this cancer, do you? That wouldn't be thinking too well of God if you're going to think that He gave it to you." "Well," I say, "I don't know that He gave it to me, but He let me have it." And we work out from that. I have a Scripture that I have lived by for many, many years that helps with this problem. Psalm 31 says: "I trust in Thee, Thou art my God. My times are in Thy hand." That means that everything that touches my life is touched by God. He puts the gift there. I look upon the things that come to me, whether they seem good or whether they seem ill, as gifts from God. I consider this pain a gift of God. I'm not afflicted by cancer. I have been honored to have this stewardship. There's but one thing to do and that's to recognize that God is a loving heavenly Father. I've come to appreciate more than ever in my life what being a child of God can be and is in our daily experience, because

God has given us *all* things. We say, "Well, He permitted it and Satan gave it." I don't care how you work it out. You've got to receive it and look up and say, "Thank you, Heavenly Father." And this touches another set of Scriptures in Paul's writing to the Ephesian church: "Always and for everything giving thanks to God the Father, in the name of our Lord Jesus Christ" (Ephesians 5:20). This is a transforming truth.

Early in my ministry I ran across a statement in the fifth chapter of I Thessalonians in which Paul said, "In everything give thanks." I remember so well how I tried to protect God by saying this: "God didn't say give thanks *for* everything, but in this scripture He said *in* everything give thanks. No matter what the situation is, be thankful in that situation." So I preached it in that manner. It wasn't too long until I ran across this other statement of Paul's written toward the end of his life: "Always and *for* everything giving thanks to God the Father in the name of our Lord Jesus Christ" (Ephesians 5:20). So we are taught in the Scripture to give thanks to God for everything. And that means *everything*. Much could be said on this scripture, but you do your own thinking and let it work out. Now, I'm in the middle of my bout with bone cancer, and I haven't changed my mind about any of it. In fact, any change in my mind has just been toward a deepening in the truth which the Lord has revealed to me, and I praise Him for it. And I try to say "Thank you, Lord" anytime anything unpleasant happens. I try to say thank you to him whether it be an unpleasant person or an unpleasant experience. God is our God and He is our Father and we are His children. We need to learn (and we can't learn any other way apparently), as the Holy Spirit reveals it to us through the Word and through the experiences of every day, that we have a stewardship and it is required in stewards that a man be found faithful.

Some two months after the doctor told me that I had bone cancer, the Sunday School lesson was from the book of Job. The big question of course that all interpreters of Job undertake to solve is the question of pain and suffering. So this particular Sunday, even the title of the lesson was, "Why did this have to happen to me?" I listened to the teacher, who did a wonderful piece of work in teaching the lesson. When he finished I thought, "I ought to get up and tell them my experience." So I got up among these more than fifty men who had known me nearly all their lives. I just told them what I've already said here in this testimony. "Here I am, at 87 years of age. I served God to the best of my knowledge and ability. I've given him control of my life. Now, here I am with bone cancer. I *could* say, 'Why did this have to happen to me?' And I can tell you this morning, gentlemen, that I think I know why it happened to me—because I understand that life is a stewardship. No matter what happens to us we are responsible to honor God with it and in it. And so I could say that all this is a gift of God and that I must take it as a gift and use it for His glory."

I went on to say some more things to those men—things that I've already written or expressed here, and when I was through, they were dumbfounded. They felt, I guess, for the first time in their lives, that God had given them a living fulfillment of some of His truths.

I'd like to close by quoting once again that poem written by Browning that has meant so much to me—"Rabbi Ben Ezra." If you don't know it, you ought to know it, and then live by it.

Grow old along with me!
The best is yet to be,
The last of life,
For which the first was made:
Our times are in His hand
Who saith, "A whole I planned,
Youth shows but half; trust God: see all, nor be afraid."

I trust that you will receive blessing as you face up to your life and your relationship with God the Father. In the name of Jesus, Amen.

19950582R00070

Made in the USA
Lexington, KY
02 December 2018